# The Shamanic
# Handbook
# of Sacred Tools
# and Ceremonies

# The Shamanic Handbook of Sacred Tools and Ceremonies

Barbara Meiklejohn-Free
and Flavia Kate Peters

Winchester, UK
Washington, USA

First published by Moon Books, 2015
Moon Books is an imprint of John Hunt Publishing Ltd., Laurel House, Station Approach,
Alresford, Hants, SO24 9JH, UK
office1@jhpbooks.net
www.johnhuntpublishing.com
www.moon-books.net

For distributor details and how to order please visit the 'Ordering' section on our website.

Text copyright: Barbara Meiklejohn-Free and Flavia Kate Peters 2014

ISBN: 978 1 78535 080 1
Library of Congress Control Number: 2015934119

A CIP catalogue record for this book is available from the British Library.

Design: Lee Nash

Printed and bound by CPI Group (UK) Ltd, Croydon, CR0 4YY, UK

We operate a distinctive and ethical publishing philosophy in all
areas of our business, from our global network of authors to
production and worldwide distribution.

# CONTENTS

# Introduction

*Imagine standing in a room with a hundred drummers. As they hold their shamanic hand drums, poised ready to journey and ride the spirit horse to new levels, you feel your heart beating fast in anticipation. You feel a little scared, frightened, but yet excited that something amazing is about to happen. Then the drums start and you feel the beat pulsating through your entire body. The connection with Spirit moves and flows deep into the very stream of your consciousness, stirring your soul's essence as it moves and shapes into a renewed, awakened life force. As the drums gain momentum they beat faster and faster and you feel yourself losing control, spinning in a vortex of energy. Suddenly you find yourself surround by animals, spirits and strange places that you have never encountered before, or have you? Something feels all too familiar. You surrender and finally relax as you sink into the depths — you have come home...*

Many may feel an affinity with the pathway of the Shaman, sensing the call. The Shaman within stirs each of us from our deep slumber. For it is time to wake up and acknowledge that the world of nature is on equal terms with humankind in keeping this planet going, as we know it. For two millennia, mankind has believed that everything on this planet is his for his own taking, to have dominion over. It is time to redress the balance and to live up to the sacred role of the Shaman. But where will this journey of mystery take you, you may ask, and where do you start?

A Shaman is someone who has always been drawn to nature, who naturally hears the whispers of Spirit through the breeze, who welcomes the rains, glorifies in the heat of the sun and connects with the nourishment of the earth. A Shaman embraces each season, rejoices at every new bud during the first stirrings of spring, the harvest abundance that summer supplies, the falling leaves of autumn and the deep dark mystery that accompanies the winter months. The Shaman's heart sings at the mere notion of the workings of Spirit, has an affinity with the ways of natural healing and believes in another world of mystical beings. The Shaman is able to naturally connect with this 'other world', perceiving the spirits that are all around, in all that is alive. This is the belief system of Shamanism, for it is not a religion, but a wonderful world of freedom, magic and connection with the natural world, and that of Spirit. Our ancestors, and other indigenous peoples, lived their lives trusting in, recognising and interacting with the spirits of the land, living in accordance with the magical law of nature. The Shaman is a healer, a counsellor and ambassador for the spirits of nature, taking a responsible attitude in guardianship for this beloved planet.

Instead of having to pick up a dozen books on the subject of Shamanism, we have combined all that the beginner needs to know into this, *The Shamanic Handbook of Sacred Tools and Ceremonies*. As you begin your path as a Shaman, of the 'one who knows', your journey will be one of remembrance as you connect with the earth-centred traditions of the ancestors.

But do not be fooled, for walking the shamanic path is a hard journey of soul-searching experiences. You may find yourself suddenly dropping everything to be on top of a mountain in some far away land, to embrace yourself in a vision quest. Or you might end up taking part in a sweat lodge or walk across hot coals in a firewalk, because you were called to be in the right place at the right time. The art is not to question, but to be ready to answer and to surrender. It will challenge you, it will push you over the edge and you may find yourself screaming that you cannot, or will not, continue. Some will walk away forever, whilst others may keep dipping their toes in, now and then. We have known people to turn their backs on Shamanism even after experiencing the most incredible feelings of ecstasy through the vibrational sounds of shamanic drums, having journeyed into the abyss of the self and healed wholly and fully, and endured heart attacks, which have lead them to an incredible connection with Spirit and their true life purpose.

The sacred pathway of the Shaman is uncertain, but necessary, if you wish to connect with the magic that is within and all around you. There may be pitfalls and great losses along the way, but you can be assured that wherever this path leads you to, the overall outcome will be more satisfactory than you could even imagine.

*Blessings,*
*Barbara and Flavia*

# 1

# Altar

Today the altar is often associated with religion. It is often a sacred space of rich, tapestried cloths, upon which lie lavish artefacts of gold in the holiest area of the place of worship where only the priest (or equivalent) has full access, to stand in the presence of God. It can be seen as a place of sacred reverence and also a place of fear, where prayers and confessions are laid bare. Altars are usually found at, and are part of, shrines, temples, churches and other places of worship and were used by ancient cultures such as the Egyptians, Greeks, Norse and the Celts. Today they are used particularly in Christianity, Buddhism, Hinduism, Shinto and Taoism, as well as in Neo-Paganism and Ceremonial Magic.

On our worldly travels we embrace the peaceful traditions of the Far East. For in every doorway, on every pathway, in corners of rooms, on beaches, rocks and even in cars are small altars, adorned with flowers and the sweet aroma of burning incense, dedicated as shrines to the spirits. This is the way of the people here, for they honour Great Spirit in all that they do, in their work, in their homes, for life itself and it is wonderful to see.

Although nature itself is an altar to the Shaman, having one's own personal altar (Thaan) helps to set one's focus for rituals, ceremonies and prayers. This is a sacred space specifically for the laying out of ritual tools, for holding pictures or artefacts of chosen deities and ancestors; a place of worship, of honouring personal beliefs and a meeting place between the ordinary and spiritual realms.

An altar doesn't have to be anything grand, so do not worry if you don't have the room in your home, or other chosen place, for anything lavish. Your altar can simply be made from a table with a cloth on it in a quiet corner, a mantelpiece, window sill or bathroom shelf. It doesn't matter so long as you have set the right intention.

You may wish to spend time creating a small space that reflects your journey and to honour the blessings and gifts given by the spirit world and Mother Nature, such as flowers, tobacco, sage, or other representations of what is sacred to you. This gift is a thank you and a pause of reflection on the gifts from the worlds the Shaman walks between.

As a Shaman you will be working with and respecting the four basic elements of Earth, Air, Fire and Water combined with the fifth element of Spirit, the life force that runs through all that is living. You will need to find items to represent each of these elements for your altar…

### To Represent the Element of Earth:
A black candle
A bowl of soil from your homeland or a sacred site
A potted plant or flowers
White Californian sage (this is cleansing and purifying; when
    lit it can count towards the Fire element too)
Crystals and stones

### To Represent the Element of Fire:
A red candle (the flame represents Fire)
A symbol or representation of the Sun

### To Represent the Element of Air:
A yellow candle
An incense stick (the smoke represents Air)
Feathers (preferably retrieved fallen feathers found in nature)
Bells
Wind chimes

**To Represent the Element of Water:**
A blue candle
Water from a holy place (such as Chalice Well, in Glastonbury,
    or a sacred spring near where you live)
A chalice/goblet (to represent the element Water or to hold
    water itself as a vessel)
Sea shells

**To Represent the Element of Spirit:**
As picture of a rainbow
A mirror
Picture or symbol of a butterfly

It is best to place the objects on your altar so that the elements correspond with their directions, with Spirit in the centre. Different traditions have their own idea about which element is associated with a particular direction. For instance the Andean tradition represents East as Fire, South as Earth, West as Water and North as Air.

Here in the Celtic lands our tradition is that North is Earth, East is Air, South is Fire and West is Water. There is no right or wrong way, so go with whatever feels good and resonates well with you. Use your creativity and intuition to make it as simple or decorative as you feel inspired. You may wish to stand a picture or two of an elemental being, the woods, a meadow, or the ocean and scatter over the surface of your altar pine cones, leaves, or what you feel drawn to use. Build whatever you feel represents the magic of nature for you. Make your altar alive and breathing with the forces of nature. Including all four elements on your altar ensures the balance in all aspects of nature, when honouring or doing all-round shamanic work.

## 2

# Amulets and Talismans

The history of amulets and talismans goes back far into the ancient worlds. They are also found throughout the world in nearly every culture such as Egypt, India, Babylonia, Greece, Rome and other parts of Western Europe, Northern Europe and America. An amulet is a symbol that is used to repel unwanted energies and brings about protection. A talisman is usually an object, such as a crystal or pendant, that is used to focus magical intentions and to bring about good luck as well as abundance, health, wellbeing and balance.

Amulets are worn or carried to imbue the wearer with the associated powers. These can be anything from the Eye of Horus, a Pentagram, the Star of David, a Crucifix, a rabbit's foot, or a four-leaf clover, depending on one's belief and culture. Amulets can also be used in the form of rings, pendants, statues, coins, pictures and even in words of prayer, magical spells and incantations to ward off and repel bad luck.

The shamanic costume is worn in some traditions. These can be ancient costumes that have been handed down from generation to generation and are believed to hold special properties and power. Sometimes the wearer will use such a magical costume to assist them in performing healing work or to undertake a shamanic journey as it ushers them into an alternative consciousness state.

We often adorn ourselves with amulets of the cultures and countries that we visit during our travels. Our favourite is the 'Evil Eye' of Turkey, which is represented in the jewellery that we wear, for it is believed to ward off negativity and enhances protection. Like many Shamans we often wear feathers, bones and shells from tribes across the world, including Northern

Thailand and Kathmandu. Barbara is never without her bear's tooth, which she wears round her neck in the form of a necklace, which was gifted to her at a Sun Dance ceremony at Wounded Knee, in South Dakota. For her it represents strength and courage, as well as protection.

Flavia has a tattoo of the Eye of Horus on her right wrist to ensure protection and to enable her to see the truth in all situations. This powerful amulet was worn by both the living and the dead in Ancient Egyptian times, to guard and protect against danger.

Every room in our house is filled with amulets and talismans. The hallway is packed with Native American and tribal artefacts such a feather headdresses, pictures, statues, masks and shamanic healing tools. We have an Egyptian room, a Constantinople room, an Eastern deities room – all dedicated to those cultures in many physical forms.

The wonderful thing about wearing and working with an amulet or a talisman to aid you in achieving your desire, is that whenever you look at it, it enforces the energy of its purpose. They are both a focus that leads you to affirm that which you believe they represent, thus aiding in amplifying your power.

# 3

# Ancestors

The power song of the ancestors called to us on our drive through New Mexico during the spring of 2013. We had driven from Phoenix to Sedona, then to Santa Fe and on to Taos. For most of the journey, along the dusty, hot roads, we could hear the chants of the spirits as they sang to us the following incantations:

*We are the old ones, we are the new ones,*
*We are the old ones from a time far away.*

*Dancing, dancing on the ancestors' bones.*
*Dancing, dancing on the ancestors' bones.*

*Sticks and stones, ancient bones*
*Calling us to bring them home.*
*Sticks and stones, ancient bones,*
*Calling us to bring them home.*

The ancestors are those who have gone before us, to pave the way so we may live a better way of life. Each year on Armistice Day and Remembrance Day millions of people stop to remember those who fought in the recent world wars, and rightly so. Sadly we aren't encouraged to remember all those who died for us long before that. For instance, how many people spare a thought for all those who were drowned, hanged or burnt to death after, wrongly, being accused of being witches? Those who died in battles fought in the name of religion? The First Nation and tribal people across the globe who were wiped out for their lands? And so it goes on. Millions of our ancestors have been lost and forgotten by those who they fought so hard to protect, their future blood generations.

Do you know who you are descended from? Are you aware of where your bloodlines stem back to and to whom?

An ancestor who has gone through the rites of transmigration (see the chapter Transmigration at the end of this book) is someone who has died a good death, having practiced and transmitted to his descendants (not necessarily bloodline) wisdom and knowledge that was passed on to them from their ancestors. They will have been a peacemaker, a sacred link of nurturing kinship between the living and the dead, through prayers and ceremonies.

Here on our British Celtic lands, Shamans practice a tradition called Samhain, commonly known as Halloween. At that time of year we honour those who have gone before us, the souls of the departed since the beginning of time, our primordial ancestors. From October 31st to November 2nd we move through into our new year, harnessing the memories of our loved ones and remembering the impact they have made in the lives of those still living.

Indigenous peoples and cultures from around the world honour their ancestors daily through ritual and ceremony. The Shaman believes that if it was not for our ancestors we would not be alive to tell the tale!

How often do you visit what was once a home of a deceased loved one? Do you visit their graves or the sacred place in which their ashes are scattered? Do you thank them on a regular basis for all they have done, whether you viewed any situations as either good or bad? Do you choose to ignore and forget them because of something they did that you dislike, or have you simply forgotten them in your daily life? Perhaps you have imagined what it must have been like for them in their day and age. How much hardship and struggle did they endure? What were their victories?

The ancestors are our spiritual kin whether we like it or not, for we chose our bloodline. This is a spiritual journey not only for us, but for the ancestors too. Remember that their actions and lives helped create and shape our own.

It is time to be in right relationship with our ancestors by honouring them daily. For in doing so we can ask for help and assistance with our own journey and spiritual work.

It is also important to realise that not only can we honour our own ancestors, but we can honour those we have encountered in previous lifetimes as well as past friends and colleagues. It is time to create an ancestral link between the living and the dead.

### Ancestor Awakening

Open your inner senses to find that it is the time of year when the veil between the worlds is thin, and you are at the water's edge at dusk. The moon shines brightly and a small boat is moored. A figure waves from the boat and invites you aboard. You soon realise that this is a friendly guide, whom you trust deeply. The boat moves out to sea towards a small island. Your guide tells you that the island is of the ancestors, and that it is quite safe.

The boat reaches the shore, and you notice a brightly coloured rainbow bridge on the land. Waiting on the other side are loved ones from whom you are descended. You step out of the boat and a guardian of the island comes to greet you. The guardian takes you to the brightly lit bridge that leads to another shore. You don't and can't cross it, but hear familiar voices and can see across to the other side. You feel an absolute warmth and feeling of love as faces you know and faces of strangers approach from the far end of the bridge. Stand towards them from your side of the bridge, and if anybody wishes to speak with you they will do so.

Spend time connecting with old loved ones, and those who came before you. Listen to what they have to say to you, and speak with them in conversation. Connect with the ancestors of others, those who have lit the way and any that have gone before you, with whom you'd like to converse. Then give thanks to those who have watched over you, left a great legacy, shared their wisdom and also give thanks for all that has gone before you.

When you have finished and said your goodbyes the guardian leads you back to the boat and you sail with your guide back into the here and now.

You may decide to dedicate a small altar with pictures of past loved ones, in honour of their memory and the connection you have with them now. For they are never far away. *'Mitakuye Oyasin'* – Lakota for, 'We are all related.'

# 4

# Ceremonies, Rituals and Initiation

Ceremonies are an expression of culture and self-worth, regarded by the ancient tribes as a way of life. For they knew that through ceremony a new life begins, in some way or other. Today, for most people, ceremonies mark a rite of passage for occasions such as birthdays, christenings, graduations, weddings, retirement and, finally, funerals. Sadly today ceremonies in assisting people to affirm their inner strengths and capabilities are not usually incorporated into our modern day living. No longer is it the norm to hold ceremonies in order to allow one to face their fears and to journey within, to listen to and know their soul. Ceremonies come from the heart centre, which speaks our truth, feels nature and enables us to become one with Creator. From here we are more able to listen to the spirits as they guide us on our individual journey in becoming whole and healed once again. We need ceremonies to awakening our inner calling, to hear the roaring that calls us to begin our journey of ceremonies; thus initiating us through each transition we embark upon during our lifetime.

Barbara grew up in the tradition of ancient ceremonies and rituals. From an early age she experienced vision quests, sweat lodges and was initiated into the Craft – as did Flavia, who was initiated into the Old Ways as a child.

We both discovered, early on, that ceremonies deepened our spiritual and healing path. For us, being without ceremonies is rather like trying to live without the very air we must breathe. It is a necessary way of life. The 'before and after' of a ceremony marks a point in our lives when we move from the mundane to the sublime. Ceremonies give us memorial structures and foundations to events in our lives. By coming together in a community, ceremonies play a powerful role in the messages they gift to us. They teach us that we are not alone – that we belong.

Ceremonies are gifted by, and come directly from, the spirits, as well as our heart centre. When we stand in ceremony we connect with nature and are one with all creation. The words that flow from our hearts speak of the moment of now and voice the feelings from everyone taking part in the ceremony.

Ritual is different from ceremony. When we perform ritual we speak from the minds of those who have devised the ritual itself. Therefore it doesn't carry heartfelt meaning, because we have been taught it. This is how it has always been done. Speaking another's words or performing their rituals loses the connection between the group. This is because those taking part are too busy focusing on the written word, re-enacting others' thoughts, actions and past deeds.

It is, therefore, so important to re-live, re-enact and to remember while taking part in ritual, with integrity. In today's world we have lost the focus of the true meaning and purpose of these ancient ways, which have been handed down in the oral tradition. By creating a ceremony we call upon the spirits; ancestors of our distant past. We call upon the wisdom to create sacred space, both within and without. Without ceremonies and rituals in our lives we lose the sense of our own culture and belief systems.

**Sweat Lodge**: An incredibly powerful ceremony held on sanctified ground where you will connect with the ancestors and Great Spirit. The heat, from fired up stone people placed in the centre of the sacred space, is immense. Through the intensity of the heat, coupled with drumming and chanting, connection is enhanced often through a state of trance.

**Vision Quest**: A wonderful ceremony to bring about your spiritual focus and answers to any questions about your path that you may have. The Shaman will often sit in nature, either on a hill or in a forest, throughout a long, dark night. It requires endurance and bravery, but will bring about connection with and answers from the spirit world directly, mostly through the sounds and visions experienced during the quest.

**Firewalking**: The act of walking barefoot over a bed of hot coal embers. It is an intense, but empowering experience, of personal transformation. Working with fire is essential to purifying the body, spirit and heart, and can be used for healing and creating fruition in our lives.

There are many other ceremonies that are available to the Shaman including drumming (see the Drums chapter in this book, for full details), as well as initiation ceremonies such as a naming ceremony, shamanic burial, death and rebirth, inner child and croning, to name but a few. Even standing within a stone circle, or in a self-created circle, can be a ceremony in itself. The key, of course, is intention!

Ceremony serves the purpose of strengthening the people, uniting them together in a sense of belonging. It's being a part of a festival, an event that focuses on the coming together, supporting and nurturing of each individual to attain their highest potential. Supporting and holding the created power of energy within the ceremony is a key focus point to change any given situation. Utilising our physical body in the act of ceremony, ignites our thoughts and ideas while uniting the realm of myth and remembrance of our soul to spark the realms of Spirit in ceremony and rituals.

## Vision Quest Journey
Imagine that you are sitting on your own in nature, next to a lake, at dusk. As you look up to the night sky you see the

15

constellation of Ursa Major, the Great Bear, twinkling above you. It swirls all around you as the bear forms right in front of your eyes.

You hear his voice saying, 'I have been called to help and sit with you on your vision quest. You have come to this most ancient of lands for regeneration and this is your chance to grow. This is a place of intensity of power, which will accelerate your abilities and gifts.

'I ask you to sit here and draw on the quality of air and to revive your spirit from the cleansing properties of the water that surrounds you. Feel the energy surge through you from the rock that you sit on as every mineral connects and rejuvenates any minerals within you that have been depleted.

'Heal, heal, heal on every level. I will accompany your night as Spirit seeks you out whilst you embark on your search. It is time to bring you back into balance of mind, body, and spirit as you are reminded of who you are. For you are the elder, the ancestor, the wise man or woman returned. You have the power, you have the gifts – time to become.'

# 5

# Cosmic Tree

To the Shaman the Cosmic Tree represents three zones of our world. The tree is seen as the central axis of the Earth (Axis Mundi) upon which the Shaman can soul-travel up to the Sky or deep down to the Underworld, in a metaphysical sense. As Shamans, we reside mostly in the Middle World of the Cosmic Tree, or the Tree of Life as it is also known. It is from here in the Middle World that the Shaman consciously embarks upon a shamanic journey. Often this is induced using rattles, drums, chants and even vision questing. This change of consciousness gives the Shaman access to the Underworld, or Lower World, of power animals and the inner depths of oneself, and upwards to the Sky, or Upper World of the Cosmic Tree, of spiritual teachers and guides. Working with these planes of existence enables the Shaman to see and understand the bigger picture of the quest, of one's life.

The Shaman understands that there is a parallel world without time or space restrictions, where spirits help, protect and teach us. The Shaman walks between both realities and works together with beings of the Otherworld, understanding that these forces and beings play a big part in our lives. We can tap into the spirit world and learn from their wisdom and knowledge as well as draw upon strength, healing and insight for ourselves and others.

The Cosmic Tree is therefore a vehicle in which the Shaman can make pilgrimage to a sacred place within the world of spirit, to go beyond the limitations of human perception.

# 6

# Crystals

Healing crystals and ancient stones have been honoured and used by medicine people, healers and Shamans since the beginning of time. Some shamanic cultures believed that the Shaman held a special crystal within his or her body and this inner wisdom was used to help and assist with journeying to the spirit world for help with healing and divination.

Crystals are gifts from the stars and are imbued with cosmic properties that we can use to help heal and connect with Spirit and our inner-selves. Crystal power appears in legends of many old and ancient civilizations. The Egyptians, Greeks, Native Americans, Lemurians and Atlanteans all used crystals in one way or another. Native Americans used crystals in their ceremonies, as did the Mayans and Aztecs because they knew of the powerful healing attributes of the stones, to aid in the healing of physical, emotional and etheric bodies.

Crystals have power to protect, to enhance, to strengthen, to uplift, to heal and as tools to interpret messages from the spirit world. Shamans believe that all of nature is alive, that all beings have spirit. Crystals are members of the mineral kingdom in the physical world. In the spiritual world they belong to the elemental realm, which encompasses the spirits that guard, heal and protect the planet. Shamans recognise this and understand that crystals are conscious partners who are happy in assisting with healings, connection work and for any form of protection.

A few years ago Flavia was horrified to discover that the local council had made plans to build a huge waste disposal site just a few hundred metres to the left of a beautiful lake that she often visited. This meant possible noise pollution, hundreds of daily visitors to the site and the general unpleasant energy that goes with it. Not nice at all for nature and for the wildlife that lived in the beautiful sanctuary of the lake and surrounding countryside. As she connected with the guardian spirits of the land she was given a vision of a crystal grid to be made specifically to keep away the energies of the 'rubbish dump', as we call it in the UK. The crystal grid would act as a barrier and energy shield, thus keeping the chaos out, and the peace of the lake in. She enlisted the help of a good friend and crystal expert, Donna, who was more than happy to help. The crystals were carefully selected and she and Donna arrived at the lake to set about laying out the grid. This had been shown to Flavia already, but where to start? They looked around and both saw, at the same time, two sticks on the ground that were laid out like a pointing arrow. They both laughed at how wonderful nature is and set the first crystal down. Now, crystals are amazing beings of spirit. Each crystal is packed with healing energy of one kind or another and are easily attuned, with intention, as they are great memory holders. These stones knew exactly what they were there to do, and so they laid them according to the plan that had been projected into Flavia's mind's eye. On completing the grid the energy was then to be transferred from crystal to crystal and then sent to an ancient burial mound a few miles away, but in plain view of the lake. Of course permission was asked of the spirit of the hill to take the negative energy and transmute it, to which of course the answer was 'Yes'!

Crystals are also used in modern day medicine and are referred to as 'piezoelectric' – meaning that electricity and sometimes light can be produced through compression. This property is harnessed in ultrasound machines, which use crystals to produce sound waves, to heal deep within the body. This is much like a rotating crystal wand on the skin, which causes compression and releases a focused beam of light/sound to the organ deep within the body. Ancient Shamans were aware of this ability of crystals and focused sound and light vibrations into a concentrated ray, which would be applied for healing.

There are many different types of crystal and each type of crystal has their own individual benefit for the Shaman healer. Crystals are available in many shapes and forms:

**Tumbled:** Rough stones in their natural state or polished stones that have been tumbled – both provide the same beneficial energies and are useful for healing arrays and holding during meditation.

**Clusters:** These occur when several crystals have grown together and are often placed in rooms to change the energy of the environment, to transform negative energy into positive. You can also cleanse smaller crystals by placing them on a large cluster and leaving them overnight.

**Spheres:** These emit a constant circle of energy, and are good to energize a room as they can reach a large area.

**Points:** These can be natural or hand-crafted. They are often used in healing layouts (or arrays). When pointed towards the body, energy is channelled in. When pointed away, energy from the body or aura is drawn out. They are excellent for constructing crystal grids for healing, clearing and protection.

**Wands:** Natural or hand-crafted, wands have the ability to focus energy through the tip and are excellent healing tools.

**Pyramids:** Artificially made and used to draw energy upwards.

**Slices:** These reveal the beauty of the stone and are an ideal aid to meditation. They can be placed in a room or on the body for healing purposes.

Different stones help with certain aspects of our lives.

**Grounding Stones:** Good protective stones for rooms, when healing someone, or for personal use are black tourmaline, hematite and smoky quartz. They have the ability to absorb negativity and give out pure clean energy.

**Malachite:** Helps strengthen the heart.

**Rose Quartz:** The 'love' stone.

**Citrine:** Known as the merchant stone, this can be kept in a purse or wallet to help bring about abundance.

**Black Tourmaline:** Used for protection, or to keep nightmares away from children.

**Obsidian:** Used for grounding and protecting.

**Fluorite:** Provides a protective shield from harmful electro-magnetic radiation.

**Amethyst:** Assists with developing spirituality and overcoming addictions. Some priests wear an amethyst ring, which is said to protect them from drunkenness!

Aware of the special properties of the crystal kingdom, the Shaman often includes these magical stones in their work as well as inviting them in as part of everyday life. It is an ancient tradition for Shamans to wear crystals on their person and there are a host of ways in which you can use and benefit from the healing energies of crystals.

**Wearing Crystals:** Wearing crystals next to the skin (as jewellery or in a bra) is one of the most effective ways to connect with and use the healing properties of crystals.

**Carrying Crystals:** They can be carried in a pouch on a belt or in a pocket. Dip your hand into the pouch from time to time to absorb the crystal's healing energy directly through your skin.

**Body Placements:** Crystals can be placed on the body on a painful or troublesome spot. They can also be placed on the chakras, which will energise and balance the natural flow of Prana within and around you.

**At Night:** Placing crystals under your pillow imparts healing benefits while you are asleep. Certain crystals can also help with insomnia, nightmares and psychic attacks as well as dream recall and astral travel. You can programme a crystal to assist with any of these.

**Drums:** Drums should come with carefully sourced and selected special crystals. We send ours direct to our Native American drum-maker Wayne, in South Dakota, where he skilfully inserts them into the handle of the hand-held shamanic drums. The crystal's energy amplifies as it resonates with the healing sound frequency of the drum, making a powerful healing for those holding or hearing the drum.

**Healing with Crystals:** This is often performed by the Shaman when undertaking practices such as soul retrieval, extraction, dream-weaving and to act as a bridge between both worlds when journeying.

**Meditating with Crystals:** This can rejuvenate both body and mind, instil inner peace and awaken insight. Crystals are a wonderful tool which the Shaman uses to help induce and enhance a meditative state of peace and tranquillity. The crystal quartz family are the most popular crystals for meditation, particularly rose, clear, smoky and amethyst. But any crystal can be used in accordance with their individual properties.

### Crystal Meditation

Take a crystal and either hold it gently, or place it on the floor or your legs, with your hands resting in your lap. Focus your attention on the crystal. Notice its beauty, its shape, form and colour. If you are holding it, be aware of its weight and feel yourself absorbing its warmth and energies.

Close your eyes and become aware of your breathing. Breathe in deeply from your abdomen, and give a long, slow exhale, blowing deliberately through your mouth. Continue breathing in this way until your mind is free from any thoughts. Now, as you breathe in, feel your body overflowing with the blissful healing energies of your crystal. As you exhale, feel any tension in your body dissolving. Allow yourself to sink deeper and deeper into a meditative state. Feel your energy field expanding and filling with beautiful, crystalline energies.

Now imagine that you are becoming part of the crystal. Allow your energy to merge with that of the crystal, becoming aware that you both have the same spirit running through your vital life force energy. Now allow yourself to enter your crystal and explore its magical kingdom. Have a look around. Feel its crystalline energy and enjoy a healing. If you wish you could ask your crystal a question and then listen for the answer. The first impression that comes to you will be your answer, whether it's in the form of hearing, seeing, feeling or knowing the crystal's response.

Remain in your blissful, meditative state for as long as you wish. When you are ready to return, become aware of your body and your contact with the earth. Gently move your fingers and toes and notice your surroundings. Take a deep breath in and slowly open your eyes.

# Directions: North, East, South, West

Many shamanic traditions observe a ritual of calling in the four directions in some form or another. This is a means of setting sacred space for ceremony, healing or invocation. It is mostly common practice to use four directions; however, some may use six or seven, depending on tradition and the land they walk upon. This goes too for the variations of directional ceremony, according to traditions of tribes.

For instance specific animals are associated with each particular direction in the Peruvian tradition. Celtic Shamans often work with nature spirits, whilst honouring Mother Earth and the elements. Many Native American tribes call upon the Great Spirit and totem animals. All traditions insist in the offering of gifts to the spirits. These can be in the sacred forms of tobacco, fruit, nuts, crystals, chocolate or anything that's deemed a suitable gift of gratitude for the bountiful blessings Spirit bestows upon us.

There are a many ways in which to call in the directions and, again, they all vary depending on heritage. Often musical instruments are played, such as drums, rattles, didgeridoos, flutes as well as some form of toning or chanting, thus uniting our hearts with the world of spirit and Mother Earth. In calling the directions we are able to focus our intentions on that which is sacred. Also, the ancestors are acknowledged and thanked for their guidance and watchfulness over our life path, as are guardians and gatekeepers of the spirit world to each specific direction. Shamans believe that they are made up of all things, of Earth, Air, Fire and Water with, of course, Spirit running through each one of us and all that is alive – thus being connected as one.

## Calling In the Directions

Create your own medicine wheel in a place sacred to you, preferably out in nature. Use stones, crystals, sticks or leaves to mark out a circle (make it as big or as small as you wish). Now draw a cross through the centre of the circle, dividing it into quarters of the four directions of North, South, East and West (making sure the quarters are facing the correct direction).

This ceremony calls in the directions as we do here on this Celtic Isle, but please call in the directions to associate with your favoured traditions and heritage of the land you are native to. So you would call forth the first direction according to which land you are on, or the season you are in. For instance if you were to hold sacred ceremony in Australia, you start with the South. Or it could be springtime in America and so you would face the East. Likewise in Scotland one would call upon the direction of North to start, and then move round the circle to East, to South finishing in the West, as portrayed in the following passage:

*The North represents the element of the Earth, the season of winter, of drawing close within, of being grounded. Here the ancestors wait to be acknowledged and to share their wisdom. The East represents the element of Air, the season of spring, of new beginnings, of creativity and putting into action one's dreams. The South represents the summer, passion, courage, love and relationships. The West represents the autumn, emotions and psychic abilities.*

Stand in each quarter in turn and, with arms outstretched, look up as you call upon the guardians of each direction, saying something like: 'I call upon the guardians and gatekeepers of the North. Keep me protected and show me what I need to release, or to freeze, in my life, in order to walk my true path. Show me the way.' Now turn to face the East and call upon the guardians and gatekeepers, asking for whatever it is that you require in relation to this direction. Continue in the same way with the South and the West and add as many words and requests as you feel inspired to, or you may simply like to hum or chant.

Do whatever feels right to you, in accordance with your beliefs and personal connection. Spend as much time as you wish to in each quarter. Become aware of how you feel in each. Which makes you feel comfortable, which do you not resonate well in?

Go deep within and allow the answers to surface. The directions will lead you and teach you well. When you have finished turn to each direction and give thanks to Great Spirit, before stepping out.

8

# Divination

Imagine Shamans sitting and gazing into the fire while beating their drums, as the rustling leaves dance all around them. As their eyes follow the sparks from the fire up into the night sky they see the clouds chasing each other in a race that ends nowhere. The winds pick up in the answer to the drums' intense beat. The river that flows beside them erupts in unity, joining in and becoming one as the air becomes spirit-filled. The spirits have heard the call and they have responded.

Shamanic divination methods have always been in use by Shamans, Seers and Oracles. Calling on the spirit in all things still helps with life's changes and challenges. But back in earlier times they would have asked questions such as, 'Will the tribe survive the winter?', 'What weather are we facing?', 'Will there be enough food this winter?'

Today most of us don't have such worries. We can shop for food in supermarkets and Google the weather forecast for the day or week ahead, but what would happen if that all disappeared? What would happen then? Too many people rely on modern technology today, which sadly governs the way of life and leads people to ignore nature's messages, which are in fact all around us.

One of the first things Swein taught Barbara was cloud divination. This form of divining is probably one of the oldest forms of divination in the world. She would sit for hours on top of the hill behind Swein's house and watch the clouds go by. She was instructed to observe the shape, the form and where the winds were blowing from. She learnt how, on a cloudy day, to perform cloud busting to focus on the sun and move the clouds away. He told her stories of the Frithirs who were the hereditary state augers of the kings of Scotland. They would stand blind-folded before sunrise on the threshold of the person's home or castle and perform an invocation. They would then make a prediction on what they saw when they removed their blindfold.

All divination methods work with nature, to ask the spirits and forces of nature for advice and knowledge. Barbara would sit for hours at the divide of the River Ness in Inverness looking for signs. She would watch fires burning and look for their teachings and observe birds flying from different directions. If a bird flew from left to right it indicated that good news was coming, and if it flew from right to left it meant that something sad was about to present itself. Vision questing is also a great form of divination to foresee visions and be inspired by Great Spirit. A Shaman ought to be aware of different types of shamanic divination, and use them as they walk between the worlds.

**Star Gazing:** The observation of the movement of stars, shootings stars and comets.

**Feathers:** This involves taking a handful of ethically/naturally sourced feathers and casting them up into the winds to see in which direction they drop.

**Fire:** To be gazed upon as pictures and shapes emerge. Watch as the smoke rises from the fire. Cast certain logs into the fire to see how they react, then when the fire dies down read messages from the ashes.

**Stones:** To be observed as you are walking on the earth beneath you. Notice the formation they take, where they are placed and how they lie on the land.

**Shells:** Cast shells onto the ground to note their formations.

**Leaves:** Particularly prevalent in autumn, leaves fall to form patterns on the ground. Even the way in which they fall is telling.

**Water:** Sit by a river, lake, stream or pond and observe how the water flows, the ripples on the water, raindrops. Watch the colours and follow the ebb and flow.

**Crystals:** To be gazed into.

**Dowsing:** This is best done using a Y-shaped wooden stick to find water and minerals.

**Animals:** From black cats crossing your path, to birds tapping on your window, animals have their own meaning and turn up with their message for you.

**Incense or Sage:** Used to watch how the smoke rises and the shapes it makes.

**Dreams:** To be recorded and interpreted.

**Runes:** Best carved in natural wood, runes are to be read.

**Celtic Ogham:** This requires going into nature and learning about the different trees. Choose wood and sticks that have fallen off the tree. Live wood can only be taken with permission from its spirit. Then make your own set, from the wood you have found, for divination purposes.

This is just a small selection of examples of natural divination. Hone in to your intuition in order to know things without being told. Start by using oracle deck cards to bring about messages. Always look at the pictures and allow clarity to come to you.

Trust your first instincts, not the nagging voice that says, 'I cannot do this, I'm making it up!'

Then apply the same principle and go outdoors. Look around you as you are driving your car. Observe the trees, the changing of the season, the birds, and then be aware of what is around you as you step out of your car. The true art of divination is to become aware of everything and everybody around you by observing, but not by being attached.

Be a way-shower! Be the one who goes out into nature, who connects with Mother Earth and read the natural signs that are staring you in the face. By noticing and receiving messages for yourself and others in this way your senses will become alive as you grow more and more sensitive to every aspect of the natural world and its magic.

# 9

# Dreams and the Dreamtime

Dreams play a big part in the shamanic way. Being able to interpret, comprehend and diagnose a person's dreams goes a long way to the healing of the whole person. By keeping a dream journal you can start to unravel and believe in the truth of your dreams and rely on them as the Celts of Britain once did. But where do dreams come from and how do they affect us from day to day, lifetime to lifetime? A great example of dreaming and dreams come from the Aboriginal comprehension of the dreamtime and its creation. The dreamtime storytellers would speak of the old time, a time when the ancestor beings emerged from within the Earth. These creators enabled us to be able to enter into the dreamtime, in order to view and access all wisdom and knowledge from the ancestors themselves.

For the aboriginals, all worldly knowledge and wisdom is accumulated through one's ancestors. What are your dreaming stories? Do you dream of past events, past lives, things that have happened a long time ago?

The dreaming mind is an expansive creative force of the entire consciousness of the universe. Past, present and the future are all one, simultaneously. There is actually no beginning or no end. It is all limitless. Once you comprehend this concept you will awaken the dormant abilities within you to be able to journey into the dreamtime and return dreaming awake.

By bringing your dreams into waking consciousness you will have made manifest, in this reality, all that is and has ever been in your entire existence. From this you will remember who you are, where you have come from and why you are here on this Earth plane right now. Your awareness and newfound perception will open the doors to becoming a shamanic dreamer.

So who were the dream interpreter Shamans who assisted both themselves and others in the active dreaming process? The earliest records of dreaming date back approximately 5,000 years ago to Mesopotamia, where they were documented on clay tablets. According to these early recorded stories the people paid close attention to their dreams. The ancients of Mesopotamia believed that when asleep the soul left the body and actually visited the places and persons that appeared to the dreamer, whilst they dreamt. It was believed that the god of dreams carried the dreamer through the dreamtime. The dream god, Morpheus, in Greek Mythology, is said to have the ability to take on human form and appeared in dreams

Antiphon wrote the first known book on dreams in the 5th century BC. Many other Greek philosophers, including Aristotle and Socrates, believed that dreams could analyse illness, predict diseases and their cures. The Babylonians and Assyrians divided dreams into the categories of good, which they believed were sent from the gods, and bad, sent by malevolent spirits or people wishing harm on the dreamer.

All ancient cultures believed their dreams were omens and prophecies from the gods. The Ancient Greeks and the Romans shared the beliefs of the Ancient Egyptians, who wrote down their dreams on papyrus, and shared their understanding of how to interpret good and bad dreams. They would induce and incubate dreams as they believed that dreaming was the best way to receive messages. The Hebrews, like many other ancient cultures, practiced dream incubation to help and support in both healing through dream interpretation, and also to use dreams as prophetic or divine inspiration to reveal events to come.

In the Bible's Old Testament, the ancient Hebrew and Christian text, it is written that the Hebrew prophet Samuel would lie down and sleep in the temple to receive the 'Word of the Lord'. It also tells of many stories of dreams with Divine inspiration. The most famous stories being that of Jacob who dreamed of a ladder stretching from Earth to the Heavens, and of Joseph, who received vivid dreams, became Pharaoh's interpreter of dreams for the whole court and saved Egypt from many years of drought and famine.

Today we go to hospitals to be healed, likewise in ancient times the Egyptians and Greeks would go to dream temples. They would bathe in special baths prepared for them, make offerings to the gods and goddesses and ask for protection before going to sleep on specially prepared beds. The following morning they would bathe again, make offerings and visit with the dream Oracles who interpreted their dreams for healing benefits and other revelations. Those who experienced vivid dreams were believed to be blessed and special.

All indigenous tribes, such as the Aboriginals and the Native Americans, believed and still believe that dreams are a way of connecting with the ancestors. This ancient art of dream weaving keeps the fabric of the universe together.

So what happened? Why did dream weaving just stop, despite it being deemed so important by pharaohs and by kings who relied on these visions so much that they would not proceed without them and their meanings? These ancient cultures knew dreams to be a direct contact with Spirit, with the ancestors. They used the visions as divination and considered them the utmost of directional guidance from the gods, in all aspects of life.

In today's world, dream weaving is a lost art. People tend to just go to sleep at night and the dream part is irrelevant. This is because society has dismissed dreams and their possible meanings. How many people experience lucid dreaming, but do not share their experience for fear of being ridiculed or from lack of awareness of its importance? Now it is considered that dreaming is something that just seems to 'happen' during the activity of sleeping, and no one is interested in what another may try to share about their dream. It's a sad fact that dreams are too readily dismissed nowadays, which was probably encouraged by religion and government, for when one understands their dreams' meanings a gateway is unlocked to the secrets of one's truth and knowing.

## Become a Dreamweaver

Before you go to bed consciously cleanse your body in the shower or bath. Light candles and treat it like the sacred ceremony it actually is, for you are preparing for the dreamtime. This is a time when most drift into an unconscious sleep, with no control of what will happen. During the dreamtime you become the soul essence of you, as you travel through time and lift time and space restrictions. Here there are no limits to the worlds you can journey to and between. Time does not exist and you are able to meet with your ancestors or future self.

Before you fall asleep place a circle of bright light around you as protection (you can do this in your mind's eye) and ask to be guided to wherever you wish to go, or to learn and discover what it is you wish to know. Keep a journal by your bed so that you can record your dreams. Look at what is happening in your life and make interpretations as to what the meanings could be for you at the time, with regards to situations and events.

Soon you will be able to be conscious in the dreamtime and direct your dreams accordingly, dreaming your dreams awake.

## 10

# Drums

*Drum sound rises on the air, its throb, my Heart. A voice inside the beat says 'I know you're tired, but come, this is the way.'*
Rumi

The spirit of the drum calls to us from the depths of the universe to remember who we are, and where we have come from. This sound of power, the sound of creation, spirals throughout the cosmos in circular vibrations, creating and destroying all in its path. Just as a black hole envelopes all, so too does 'Nada Bindu', the primal sound from which the world was created. Everyone has the ability to connect to this sound and with it create or destroy our personal worlds.

What we are seeking, on profound subconscious level, is the sound that is responsible for all of creation to manifest. How can we access that which we disconnected from? How can we connect to that pure resonance that takes us into the state of bliss? What will ignite the inner fire of those ancient memories and return us once again to the state of Nirvana? It is the beat of the drum that connects us back to our memories and feelings of our own mother's heartbeat, to the Cosmic Mother, the ancient recollections of rituals and ceremonies that we once celebrated from prehistoric times. It is the sound, energy, vibration of the spirit of the drum that can awaken our lost primal sound, the sound of our soul. It is the spirit of the drum that is waiting to sing our souls back home...

Hand-held frame drums have been around for thousands of years. They are one of the oldest known sacred musical instruments along with the flute (dating back to 43,000 years ago and made of mammoth tusk ivory), pipes, rattles and the lyre, as well as the gong of ancient China, the sistrum of ancient Mesopotamia, Egypt and Anatolia and the didgeridoo of the indigenous 'Australians' going back 1,500 years.

Records from history and archaeological findings give us these facts, such as the mammoth tusk flutes found in a cave in Southern Germany in 2009, and the excavations in Mesopotamia that unearthed small cylindrical drums dating back to 3,000 BC. Our ancestors left us clues, which can be found through the wall reliefs of Anatolia, depicting men and women drumming in what appears to be an ecstatic trance and dating back 6,000 years, and drums that were found amongst the treasures in the discovered ancient tombs of Egypt.

The reliefs in the Shrine Room of the Neolithic site of Catal Huyuk, in Turkey, depict drawings of figures in a shamanic ritual, appearing to dance, chant and drum. Imagination can be used with these drawings to understand and see how the women and men used these instruments to invoke the spirits in assisting with hunting and the fertility for good crops. If we look back at Biblical times, the Book of Exodus states that Miriam, sister of Moses, was playing the frame drum, called the Toph, while the women rejoiced in trance over the miracle of the parting of the sea (Exodus 15:20). In the Bible it is also written that the frame drum, along with other musical instruments, was used to sing and praise the Lord (Psalm 150).

Drumming is one of the most ancient tools of communication and healing, and of ways of praying. The frame drum was, and still is, the instrument that invokes trance states. It could be for this very reason that throughout the world's history it has been feared by priests, governments, and religions. The reason the drum can threaten is because it has the ability to reconnect humankind back to our true nature. Drumming empowers us to rediscover who we really are and where we have come from through the mists of time.

Even though the references to drums are in the Old Testament of the Bible, they were not included in the New Testament and were removed by the early Christian worshippers. This is because of the drum's association with the Divine Goddess, worshipped by the old matriarchal religions. References to the womb, full moon and anything connected with the female Earth-based traditions were suppressed by most of the subsequent patriarchal religions that originated in the Middle East.

What is the fear of women and drumming? Let's look at what the ultimate gain is through drumming. We know, from our own experiences, that when we connect with the drum and play it that there is a dramatic change of consciousness, which invokes ecstatic trance and transformation. We connect with the spirit of the drum, and find that the drum actually plays us, ultimately leading us to a place of full connection with the Divine and accessing our soul.

Let's go back to the early Christian days. These were times when it was important for the new religion to conquer old practices and on November 8th of the year 392 the Emperor Theodosius abolished the freedom to practice all pagan cults. The Old Ways were all about worshipping the Divine Goddess in all her glory and because of this women had been adorned and respected throughout Pagandom, which was most of Europe and beyond. The new religion's church responded by barring women from vigils and in the year 826 they prohibited women from singing, dancing and public speaking. This was a new collective consciousness that was so fearful that something must have happened in history that has not been written about. Women were urgently dismissed of who they really are, as though their power had to be squashed immediately. At the same time, prophesy and divination were banned, as was drumming and the playing of instruments, like the tambourine that was outlawed by Pope John III in the 6th century. This wasn't feared by these men of authority because of not knowing how powerful these ways were, it was because of the fear of allowing the people to be able to connect directly with Source. The church was a newly formed council of men who would do anything in their power to put a stop to anyone being able to access that direct channel. They decided that the only way to 'God' would be through them, their new establishment, and so would set up a whole new way, impart a new religion, to put it into place for the world to adhere to.

So instead of using the drum for trance, journeying and raising consciousness to connect with the spirit world it was instead to be used to instil respect for authority, out of fear. The drum beat was used for all forms of execution and war; it would be the last thing a condemned person would hear before they passed over. Sadly the drum triggers fear in many people to this day, as the memory of the sound of the drum, before impending death, has accompanied them through to this lifetime.

During the Transatlantic Slave Trade, the African people were not allowed to take drums when being shipped to the New World. Each African had a natural and deep connection with their drum and felt it contained their own personal spirit. Being without their drum was like having their spirit snatched from them. More sinisterly, however, drums were used on the ships by those in authority to beat out the rhythm of the rowing sequence that the slaves had to adhere to, which took them to their final destination.

Today drums of varying shapes and sizes are found in every culture; Native American Pow Wows, playing at Egyptian weddings and Hindu and Buddhist ceremonies, the Japanese art of Taiko drumming, the Irish bodhran and the drum-kit of popular music.

By connecting with the ancient instruments, which have been played since the beginning of time, we become part of the wise and ancient traditions spanning thousands of years.

(For a more in-depth history of drumming you may like to read *When the Drummers were Women* by Layne Redmond.)

## Meditation Journey

Before we venture further into working with the drum we feel it is important to honour those drum keepers who have gone before us. These are the ones who kept the spirit of the drum alive, even in the face of adversity, who we give our thanks and gratitude to. For without them the wisdom and the knowledge would not have survived to this day. We are going to acknowledge these ancestors now.

So, find a quiet place where you won't be disturbed and listen to a CD of gentle shamanic drumming (see the back of this book for details of where to acquire one), or play the two beat on your own drum.

Take a deep breath, close your eyes and focus on the sound of the two beat of the drum. Allow yourself to drift with the sound and vibration of the two beat, back through time, until you come to a place that feels familiar to you. In your mind's eye, you become aware of a ceremony in process and you observe a vibrant procession with drums, dancing and chanting. You join in the procession and get swept along with the singing and drumming. Notice the people around you, become aware of your surroundings. This is a joyous celebration of life, as you see the people with offerings of baskets of flowers and fruits. There is much laughter as you are carried along the procession which leads you to a huge, white marble temple, floors adorned in the scattering of bright and colourful flowers.

At the entrance of the temple you feel a deep reverence as you bow your head, and step bare-footed over the threshold. Inside you marvel at the sight of the beautifully decorated ceilings above you and huge pillars that surround you, and with a relieved sigh you realise that you are home. A cheer comes up and as you look through the crowds you see the priestesses carrying a resplendent statue of the goddess Cybele. As she is placed down gently before you, you notice the crown upon her head and the frame drum in her left hand. And you gasp as you remember... this is the goddess of the drum! And in that moment of remembrance a drum beat strikes up – and you hear the following incantation being chanted loudly:

*Goddess of the Drum*
*To you, in awe, we come.*
*We ask to be reminded.*
*Of how it was begun...*
*Moons ago when we were free,*
*To connect and truly be.*
*Through the drum beat, to the Source.*
*Awaken now our recourse,*
*To share the wisdom and the truth,*
*That was taken by many, from our youth.*
*I stand upon this sacred place*
*With drum in hand, a smile on face,*
*To change what has gone before.*
*To re-write wrongs for evermore.*
*Give me the strength to take a stand,*
*And drive this power across the lands.*
*For all to feel as one with sound*
*Is through the drum, it's what you found.*
*The access to the Whole and One,*
*Is through the sacred spirit of the drum.*

As you stand before Cybele be aware of any emotions and feelings that may be surfacing. This is a time for you to look at when and why you may have been stopped from singing, dancing and drumming. What or who stopped you from expressing your soul, from connecting with the Divine?

Allow the answers to flow to you as you open your heart to her. She understands and thanks you for reconnecting with your deep resonance of the drum. You give your thanks to Cybele and a priestess leads you back through the temple to an outside courtyard and points to a shrine of tombs.

As you walk amongst the beds of the ancestors you become aware of the beat in your heart, which appears to get stronger as you step towards a grave that bears familiar words upon its headstone. You kneel at its side and as you read the words the beat of your heart slows down to one of comfort, for the name emblazed upon the stone is yours.

This is the resting place of who you once were, of where you received dream oracles as an initiate for Cybele, freeing you from the fear of death. Do you remember? You, who through secret mystery rites performed with the drum for the goddess Cybele and connected many others with the rhythm of life. This was your resting place, in an ancient time, a burial with your beloved drum that has always been part of you and you with it. The connection you have had, with this ancient instrument of the Divine, has been played out in many subsequent lifetimes, through incarnations of joy and those of hardships. But always throughout you were, and still are, the keeper of the wisdom of the drum.

The drum is here now to remind you of your relationship with it, and it with you. Its place is to awaken your soul to who you really are. So allow your being to be rekindled with the spirit of the drum as you journey with the beat...

Once you have finished your journey, take a deep breath and place the soles of your feet firmly on the ground to re-connect you with the here and now, and give thanks.

Cybele is an Anatolian, Greek and Roman mother goddess and protector who was celebrated through wild and outrageous processions accompanied by chanting and the music of flutes, sistrums, cymbals and, of course, drums. She had a disorderly and ecstatic following that was known to be the utmost route to connection with the Divine. Sadly, when the Roman Empire conquered with the 'new' religion, her temple, the Phrygianum in Rome, was destroyed and was re-built as the Vatican. But her spirit lives on – through the spirit of the drum.

## Making or Choosing a Drum

*Every drum is awaiting its destined keeper to awaken it into the world of sound and vibration, to give it a name, a purpose and meaning.*
Barbara Meiklejohn-Free

Since Barbara's first visit to All-One-Tribe drums, she has worked with many people who collaborate to make drums. When a drum-maker begins his next frame, or an artist is inspired to paint a vision on a drum skin, they know the finished creation is destined for the one person that the drum has been waiting for.

There is no coincidence that you have picked up this book. Either you own a drum or the drum is calling to you. There are many ways of choosing your drum, or better still, allowing the drum to choose you. This may come in a vision, a dream or a calling. You can be led on a physical journey to find your drum as she did (full story can be found in *The Shaman Within* by Barbara Meiklejohn-Free, published by Moon Books) or it may be gifted to you. Drums can be purchased by merchants of shamanic wares, or you make take the opportunity to make your own during a drum-making workshop. Once you have been partnered with your new drum, paint your totem, or communicate your vision to an artist to transfer your vision onto the skin of the drum.

When Barbara worked at the Arthur Findley College she was eager to demonstrate the amazing drums she had brought back with her from America. One of the course organisers, Brenda Lawrence, was keen to see the new collection. Later that week Barbara invited Brenda to her business showroom where she had displayed the whole new range. Before Brenda arrived Barbara wrote Brenda's name on a piece of paper and placed it under the turtle drum, which Spirit had assured was the one waiting for her. Brenda was greeted by 20 drums face up, showing off all the newly painted designs. She did not touch any of them before closing her eyes and then asked Spirit to guide her to the drum that was waiting for her. When she opened her eyes, she pointed immediately to the turtle drum and declared, 'That is my drum!' Barbara asked her to go to the drum and pick it up, and of course there she found her name written under it. She smiled and admitted that she had asked Spirit to merely confirm her knowing as she was sure that she had heard the turtle drum call to her upon entering the room.

Being chosen by your drum is an easy process, if you have the courage to trust in the calling. But choosing what you feel suits you could take longer for there are many types and shapes of drums. The variety of frames can be round, six- or eight-sided or oval and made of wood, metal, or plastic.

This is the stage to know how important it is to find a reputable drum-maker, such as Wayne and Gerry in South Dakota who have been making drums for Barbara for more than 20 years. Red Bird, from Cochiti Pueblo, who comes from a long line of family drum-makers taught Barbara, many years ago, that it was very important to ask questions when buying a drum, such as, 'Who made it?', 'Where is the skin and wood from?', 'Are the materials ethically sourced?'

Those of you who have made your own personal drums will know how important this is and not to just pick up a drum from a run-of-the-mill factory in the likes of Indonesia. We have seen them thrown together by people who have no comprehension or understanding. To them it is a product and not a sacred tool. When we make our own drum, or purchase from someone like Wayne and Gerry, you are assured that during the making process personal prayers are said, dedications are made to the drum and its spirit is invoked. It is important to be aware of the history and the properties of the materials that are used.

## Framed Wood

There are many types of woods for the frames and hoop. Here are some of the meanings for them and why you may be connected with a particular wood:

**Cherry:** Represents spring, new beginnings, death and rebirth, sacred, the Far East, fragility, way-shower, fertility and growth, beauty, peace. Essence of a human's short life, well lived.

**Walnut:** This is about longevity, aphrodisiac powers, love, fertility, growth of the spirit. Abundance in one's life.

**Ash:** Relates to higher awareness, sensitivity, expansion, power, magnitude, soul growth, the connection between Earth and Sky (Heaven and Earth), resurrection and renewal, wisdom and surrender.

**Cottonwood:** The sacred tree of the Sun Dance, spiritual growth, awakening, vision of the truth, prayers, blessings, purity, hope, communicating with the spirits.

**Rosewood:** Offers healing, love, prayer, enlightenment, knowledge of spiritual matters (good for wands too!)

**Maple:** Symbolises nations, strength, positivity, the emblem of lovers, peaceful dreams, keeper of children.

**Cedar:** The tree of protection, healing, cleansing, purification, truth, timber of the gods, smudging.

**Pine:** Balances strength with softness and mind with emotions. It is the remover of pains and fears through its foresight and removes guilt and pain on an emotional level. It heightens psychic sensitivity and prevents manipulation and influence of others.

**Birch:** Tree of the goddess, summer time, Beltane. This is one of the three trees of the pillars of wisdom. It represents creativity, youth and beginnings, wards off the evil eye; offers safety, security, clearing out of negative energy and is a protector of newborns.

**Chestnut:** Foresight, knowledge of journeying between the worlds. This wood is sustaining, nurturing, promotes well-being, balance of mind, body and spirit, longevity, invigoration of the soul, fertility and abundance. Touching the chestnut energetically draws out of the wood the invigoration and longevity of the tree's spirit.

**Beech:** Ancient knowledge, prosperity, good luck. It is a tree of learning and wisdom, healing and connection with the Earth. It is also a connector between us and the spirits.

Trees represent the Earth element; the rim of the drum, made of wood, represents the bridge between the Upper World and Lower World. Trees are the wisdom keepers, they are the standing ones of the Earth. The trees are the guardians of the Ogham, the ancient Druid tree alphabet, which the cycles of time were deemed to be connected to. Trees grow in the Earth, the ground, and are nurtured by the elements of Earth – whilst Water/rain, Fire/sun, Air/wind and Spirit seeds them.

Trees play a symbolic role in human psychology and religion. The Tree of Life (or Cosmic Tree) is found throughout many different cultures, and of which the Celtic Tree Oracle is a system of divination. Trees have fed us, kept us warm and we use them in our everyday lives still, in medicines, teas, poultices and tinctures. They gift us with oxygen and offer us shelter, healing and protection. How many people overlook the importance of these mighty and powerful allies that we share this planet with, and which contribute to our very survival?

## Skins

Different types of skins can be used for the covering of the drum, and each animal that is chosen has a different medicine (energy) which is imbued into the drum itself:

**Deer:** Covers love, grace, peace, beauty, fertility, humility, generosity and good fortune. It is associated with the moon, the dawn and Easterly direction. Ask deer to go within to seek out your inner treasures. Deer always knows where to find the best herbs and medicines.

**Cow:** This animal is considered sacred in many traditions. It refers to fertility, nourishment, nurturing, abundance, power. Ask cow for patience and connection to Mother Earth.

**Goat:** About climbing to great heights, symbolising spiritual achievement and ambition, reaching to one's highest potential, patience, perseverance, courage, balance, vitality, experience. Ask goat to be able to sample a bit of everything in order to know more deeply the world around you.

**Buffalo:** Invites you to give of everything, inspiring interconnection, strength, stability, prosperity, abundance. Ask buffalo to see the vision of the greater whole. Buffalo poses the question, 'Do you respect all that you have been gifted?'

**Horse:** Encompasses companionship, grace, beauty, freedom and strength. Horse is a messenger, helper and harbourer of spiritual knowledge. Ask horse to ride you into the world of spirit.

**Elk:** Covers abundance, plenitude, strength, endurance, pride, majesty, agility, freedom. Ask elk to help you to pace yourself, without burning yourself out. Elk brings awareness and encourages observation of what's occurring in your life.

**Bear:** All about introspection, solitude, intuition, protection, independence, self-sufficiency, rest. Ask bear to assist in allowing yourself to retreat and look within. Bear brings about stability and reliability.

**Moose:** Speaks of unpredictability, spontaneity, confidence. Ask moose to raise your levels of self-esteem and worth. Stand proud!

Skin represents the Water element, as without water our skins would dry out, for moisture feeds the skin. It is important when choosing your drum to be aligned with, or to learn from, the skins that it is covered with, for skins are infused with the spirit of the animal (medicine energy) they come from.

Many people are drawn to have their totem animal (power animal, animal guide), a plant, sacred sign or symbol that they are drawn to, or for protection, painted onto their drum. In this way the spirit of the chosen totem is imbued into the drum, enabling its energy (medicine) to emerge when played. Totem designs on the drum represents the element of Air, which carries the spirit of the totems to the people.

You can have several animal guides throughout your life. Each will come in at a specific time for you, when you are ready for, or need them for a current situation. If you are unsure of which totem you should paint on your drum look back at which animal has played a big part in your life, or what you are drawn to. Perhaps for a clue have a look around your house and observe any pictures, ornaments or books that may feature a particular animal. This could be the way that the spirit of that animal is calling to you. When searching in this way pay particular attention to the dreamtime. You could ask Spirit, before going to sleep, for your animal guide and protector to come into your dreams and show themselves.

Ten years ago Barbara had agreed to display 20 drums along with flutes, feathers, sage and jewellery at a Mind, Body, Spirit show in Manchester, UK. While packing for the show Barbara went to her vast drum collection and asked Spirit which drums were to go to Manchester with her. Immediately a drum painted with a wolf on top of a mountain told her that it was ready to go 'home'. So she packed the drum in its case, and selected more drums, to make up the 20, to accompany the wolf for the show.

On the second day of the event, a young lady approached her and said she had a dream of a wolf coming to visit her the night before. She was told by the wolf in her dream that a drum was waiting for her. Upon awakening she absolutely knew that she had to visit the Mind, Body, Spirit show that day in Manchester. She confided in Barbara that she knew nothing about drumming, but just knew without a doubt that she had to have a drum. The young lady spoke of how she had always seen wolves in the dreamtime, and was aware that wolf was her power animal. She had spotted the wolf drum, which was displayed high on a wall with the other 19 painted drums that could be seen from quite a distance, and created a beautiful sacred space.

As the drum was handed to her she confirmed that it was the same wolf that had come to her in the dreamtime. She held the drum to her heart before inspecting it more closely and sobbed as she pointed to the artist's name, 'Alison', written in the bottom corner. The woman now holding the drum declared, between sobs of joy, that her name too was Alison. She knew that, without a doubt, this drum was hers and that she had answered the calling of the drum that was foretold to her in the dreamtime.

When using the drum we are drawing on the essence of our soul. It is the element of Fire that represents and connects us back to our soul's passion and spontaneity.

The fifth element, Spirit, is the spirit of the drum, which has lain dormant waiting to be awakened by you. Your drum is your voice, heart and soul, it is the spirit of life. So make love to your drum as you play together, become your drum. Each person has a different soul note, a resonance (frequency) of the cosmic Aum, and so does each drum. No two drums are the same, nor do they talk the same. No two people can drum the same drum with it sounding the same. The drum will always choose the person and be a calling, for the drum knows its caretaker and vibrates to their 'partner's' tone and pitch, as your tone and pitch will vibrate to that of your drum.

There are different drums for different work, for example a synthetic drum is an ideal shape-shifting drum. Many people use Remo drums. They are made from Mylar/Fibreskin, and are modelled on the Native American style of frame drums. These drums are called Buffalo drums. We prefer to call them shape-shifting drums due to their ability to take on energy in any given situation. Even though they are made from non-natural materials, you can still call on their spirit, and imbue your own spirit to fuse the energy into your drum. Synthetic drums are ideal to use in cold, damp and high humidity atmospheres, such as sweat lodges.

Natural skins are prone to losing the required tension for drumming in these atmospheres. Synthetics are great for holding up in all weather conditions, unlike natural skin drums, which can change their tone and voice quite dramatically.

As there are many different drums, there are also different drum handles. For example you can have a beautiful stone or crystal imbued into the hide of the handle, to assist you in your healing work. In the same way that your spirit fuses with that of the drum, so too will the spirit and energy of the stone or crystal. Others may choose to have a handle made out of antlers, to connect with that animal's medicine, and some find a certain type of wood that they feel drawn to work with. It's all about personalising your drum, so you may find that you want to include feathers, bells, charms and such like to accompany you and your drum on your journey together.

Drum beaters or sticks are best made from wild chokecherry wood. It needs to be as natural as possible and is just as important as the drum. The beater is your physical connection when playing with the drum and represents the 'female', whilst the drum represents the 'male'. Again, the essence of your spirit is imbued into the beater, as it is in the drum, and is a facilitator of your personal power. Personalise your beater, as you would your drum by tying feathers, weaving your hair, or ribbon around it.

Different beaters have different sounds, as do the many varieties of skins. For example a buffalo skin has a thicker and lower resonant tone than that of deer skin. So again, it is really important to try out a variety of beaters, as well as drums, to find the right one for you.

Once you have found your drum and beater it is vital that they are cared for properly. Protect them in a proper drum cover or wrap them in a medicine blanket to keep warm.

As mentioned earlier, drums made of natural materials (rawhide) are extremely susceptible to changes in temperature and humidity. These drums should be oiled every couple of months with either olive oil or neatsfoot oil (available from good equestrian stores) to prevent cracking or splitting. You must apply the oil very lightly with a cloth on all parts of the rawhide, front and back. The following guidelines should be observed for caring for your drums:

**In the Car:** Never leave your drum in direct sunlight. Find a shady spot in the car and/or cover the drum with something impenetrable by the sun, or take the drum with you in your drum bag.

**In the House:** Do not store your drum near a heater, stove or fireplace or in direct sunlight. Your drum needs to be stored in a room with a constant temperature, somewhere there are no heating appliances that will dry out your drum.

**On the Wall:** This is the best place to hang your drum. Do not leave it on the floor, and choose a spot away from heating vents, fires etc. Extreme heat causes natural oils to evaporate and may cause the hide to crack.

**In a Sweat Lodge:** Not advised. Extreme moisture in the sweat lodge will cause the drum to lose its tone and the hide will become very soft and out of shape. Be warned that when this happens it will not return to its original, tight state. The wood of the frame drum will also warp, causing irreparable damage. It is suggested that a synthetic drum, such as a Remo drum, is used during a sweat lodge. This way you can be sure that your drum keeps its tone and shape throughout. It is the prayers and intentions that are most important, so do not worry about the synthetic element of your drum. Never leave it lying outside on the ground as moisture will seep into the drum. If you do place your drum anywhere keep the drum facing upwards i.e. handle to the earth; face of the drum to the sky.

**Around Campfires:** Heat from a fire will quickly cause the hide to tighten and the tone to rise. Be careful though as prolonged exposure will cause the hide to crack, and when this happens the drum is damaged beyond repair.

**On a Trip:** Always remember to cover your drum with either a drum bag, soft material or a blanket when you are travelling. A drum is for life – please take care of it.

### Awakening the Spirit of the Drum Ceremony

This ceremony should preferably be done outdoors. You will need to gather representations of the five elements:

Earth to represent the drum – collect some soil from a land sacred to you; Water to represent the skin – fill a vessel to hold the water, or place yourself near a stream, ocean, river or lake; Fire to represent the passion of the soul – a lit candle or fire; Air to represent the totem – a feather and a smudger (such as sage or incense stick); Spirit – you will be invoking the spirit of the drum.

Your ceremony should be performed when the veil is at its thinnest, when the sun is coming up at sunrise or going down at sunset. At your chosen time take your drum to a comfortable, safe place that is sacred to you, in nature if possible. It is important to use the most natural settings and tools you can. If you are in a building, such as your home, then obviously safety comes first. So, for example, light a candle to represent the element of Fire, rather than lighting an open log fire in the middle of a room.

When you have chosen your space it is time to create a sacred circle. You can do this by using bird seeds to make the shape of a huge circle around you, or use drops of water, pebbles, stones or anything from one of the elements that you are drawn to use (again, remember safety first).

Within the circle divide it into quarters. This can be achieved be marking out a cross with your chosen marker (pebbles, seed, etc). Each quarter should face one of the four directions (North, East, South, West), and each element represents one of the four directions.

In the Celtic lands we use the following representations;

Earth represents the North, Air represents the East, Fire represents the South and Water represents the West. (Note: whichever land you are on use the directions and elements that are of your traditions.) Place each element that you have collected in its relevant directional quarter.

Now take your drum and stand in the North quadrant, facing that direction. Take some of the earth into your hand and gently rub it onto your drum and say the following words, *'I offer my drum to the element of Earth. Grant me safe passage and give it birth. Anchor and hold me as I journey through, with my drum playing on, I ask this of you.'*

Now with your beater play the one beat slowly and purposefully as the element of Earth imbues its spirit into your drum. (Full instructions on drum beats can be found on *The Spirit of the Drum* CD by Barbara Meiklejohn-Free.) Now, step into the direction of East. Use your feather, lit incense or sage stick, your tool representing the element of Air, to smudge and purify the air around your drum, whilst saying the following the words, *'I offer my drum to the element of Air, to cleanse and clear me so I can share, the sacred gifts this drum offers me of inspiration, visions and creativity.'*

Now with your beater play the two beat slowly and purposefully as the element of Air purifies your spirit with that of the drum.

Now step into the direction of the South.

With your lit candle, or fire, sweep the drum over the flame (making sure not to get it, or you, too close to the flame) and say, *'I offer my drum to the element of Fire. Open the passion of my heart's desire, ignite my internal burning flame, so my true soul, I can proclaim.'*

Now with your beater play the three beat however your passion leads you.

Now step into the direction of the West. Scoop the water with a hand and allow droplets to fall onto and cleanse your drum and say, '*I offer my drum to the spirit of Water. Align my emotions, help them to alter, responses to feelings, help me to heal my senses and reason to what I can feel.*' Now with your beater play the four beat fervently, feeling every response from the drum to your beat.

Step into the centre of the circle and start chanting, '*Earth, Air, Fire, Water... Return! Return! Return! Return!*' Repeat the calling many times as you create the energy build-up of each element to rise. Visualise the element of each direction flowing through you as you call upon the spirit of the drum, whilst using the one beat.

Now call upon the element of Spirit. Chant three times as you take the beater, hitting the skin in representation of the sacred marriage of the female (beater) and male (drum), '*Spirit of the drum I call to thee, spirit of the drum come to me. Spirit of the drum I pledge to thee, hear my words and set me free. Awaken my spirit as you sing me home. For with you, dear friend, I am ne'er alone. Together we journey, to our place home, one heart, one voice, one soulful tone.*'

Now allow the rhythm of the drum to flow through you as the drum drums you.

When you are led to stop drumming take the drum to your heart (the drum's face towards the heart) and breathe in its spirit. Merge with it as one. Enjoy and feel the connection. When you a finished, give thanks and step out of the circle, through the North (gate) direction. Take with you your tools, and extinguish any burning flames. You may wish to sleep with your drum, for more connection and meetings in the dreamtime.

### Exercise: Personalise Your Drum

Connect with the elements as you gather sacred ingredients to personalise your relationship with your drum. A crone bag, or medicine bag, can simply be a piece of leather tied with string or ribbon. This is a vessel for all that represents your personal power, strength and anything that has meaning to you when connecting with Spirit, and your drum. You may fill it with pebbles or stones collected from different sacred sites (although do first check with the owners of the sites if you are allowed to take stones), dried flowers from favourite nature spots, feathers left by birds that have meaning to you or a variety of crystals. In the same way you may like to weave feathers around your drum or beater handle, add beads, crystals, jingle bells and stones to it and attach your medicine bag into the drum to really cement your relationship with your personal power and sacred medicine. Finally, take your drum to your heart and call on Spirit to bless the drum and drummer as one, place your intention as you hold that sacred space.

# Elements

Shamans around the world work with the four basic elements of Earth, Air, Fire and Water. They recognise that without these elements our world would not exist, and without the fifth element of Spirit, nothing would be alive. Each of the elements are necessary for human life, and without them this planet would be lifeless. The elements work in harmony to create and to sustain life, even though at times it can seem otherwise. The elements are from the natural world and by working with them we become more aware of our connection to nature, to our place in the world and how all things seen and unseen are needed to make up the universe.

We work with the elements knowing that each has its own representation and component of Divine energy. We can pull that energy through in accordance to what is needed in ritual, spiritual, personal work and ceremony. Many traditions associate these elements with the cardinal directions; North, East, South, and West as well as to the seasons of winter, spring, summer and autumn. Working with the elements brings about the energy of which each represents, as the Shaman harnesses that power into their sacred workings.

In our shamanic tradition here in the UK, the element of Earth is in the direction of the North, it is the time of midnight, and the season of winter. This is a time when nature goes deep within itself to rest and recharge. The Earth nurtures and restores all that reside in her, as she brings about her gifts that are steeped in magic and mystery. Earth connection helps us to maintain our logic and common sense and keeps us grounded and stable.

Air is in the direction of the East, it is the time of dawn, and the season of spring that brings about freedom and new beginnings.

The magic of Air stimulates the power of the mind, enhances the intellect and brings about mental clarity. Air offers us aspiration; inspiration and creativity find their place here. Fire is in the direction of the South, it is the time of noon, and the season of summer. The magic of Fire brings about lust, passion, attraction, illumination, love, sex, sun, warmth and inner power! Fire can be our motivating driving force, giving us strength and courage and fuelling our passion for life.

In shamanic terms Water is the time of dusk. It is the direction of West and is the season of autumn, where nature starts to turn within itself and we reflect on where we have been, what we have done in the preceding months. The element of Water helps us to achieve balance, harmony, inner peace, tranquillity and to unwind. Water governs our emotional wellbeing and assists in developing our intuition and psychic abilities.

It is so important to find out for yourself how each of the elements and directions feel for you. Go out into nature and face the direction of the North, for instance. Check in with how North feels to you. Are you comfortable as you connect with the element of Earth? Does it feel natural to want to go deep within or do you feel an awkward connection, maybe one of fear? If so, ask yourself, why? Journey into that feeling and discover your truth about the situation.

The Shaman familiarises themselves with the characteristic traits of the elements and spends time getting to know themselves in relation to each element. It's a wonderful way of discovering what aspects may be lacking or need honing within you, that you may need to bring into your healing work, or into your life in general. If you feel that you want to connect with a particular element then take time to do so.

A wonderful shamanic way to connect with the element of Earth is to have a burial. This very suggestion is often received with great fear. However, it is one of the best forms of death and rebirth that a Shaman can undertake, as a physical representation of this ancient rite of passage. If you feel that you would like to experience this element in another way then just get out into nature and take your shoes off. Allow your feet to sink into mud, or feel the damp soil beneath you and allow the earth to nourish you. You may wish to start gardening or tend to potted plants. Sit on the ground and imagine roots, from the base of your spine and the soles of your feet, growing and reaching down into the ground. Feel rooted and rest within the arms of Mother Earth for a while.

There is no better way to connect with the aspirational aspects of the element of Air than to stand on a hill on a blustery day. Shamans who work with Air know instinctually which direction the wind is blowing from. When you get to recognise patterns of the wind you become attuned to this inspirational element of creative thought and meditation. If you feel you'd like to develop this airier side of yourself then take a parachute lesson, sky dive, go on a roller coaster ride or simply go for a walk and embrace the element of Air that whispers to you on a breeze as it caresses your face.

Acquaint yourself with the element of Fire by visiting a hot climate, walk bare-footed across hot coals at a supervised firewalk or gaze at the flame of a candle or those of a wood fire and feel that connection. The sun is the greatest example of the element of Fire, and which many ancient cultures worshipped. For example, the Egyptians saw the sun as the god Ra. Today many of the remaining Native American Tribes perform a Sun Dance each year to honour the sun as the bringer of life.

You may wish to connect with the purifying elements of Water. When we take a bath or a shower we immediately receive the healing and cleansing benefits of water, both physically and metaphysically. Sign up for swimming sessions at your local pool, visit a beach and connect with the ocean, swim with dolphins, drink more water and become conscious of its positive qualities.

You will find that as you work with, and come to understand, these forces of nature you bring your life into balance and develop a greater understanding of the world around you.

# Feathers

In Celtic traditions feathered robes were worn in ceremony by the Druids to invoke the sky gods. The Ancient Egyptians and Aztecs believed also that feathers were symbolic of the sky gods. Birds were looked upon as spirit messengers whose feathers were used in ceremony and ritual. This remains true to the Shaman today for feathers represent Spirit, truth, ascension and flight. In the Native American Indian culture feathers represent the power of the Thunder Beings; the air and wind. In their culture the Native Americans believe that birds represent spirit guides. So when different birds or feathers come in their path they are believed to have come as teachers or guides. Feathers are kept and used to decorate prayer sticks, pipes and head-dresses as a way of keeping the energy of what is believed the bird represents. Feathers are seen as a three-way connection between those who have been presented with one, the bird from which the feather came and the Creator. A feather was awarded to brave warriors who fought in battle. This is why chiefs were adorned with feathers in their head-dresses, for they were seen as the strongest and bravest of them all.

Fallen or falling feathers are seen as messages from the spirit world. They are perceived as a gift from nature when they arrive unexpectedly in one's path. If you are gifted with a feather, sit with it and then ask the spirit of the bird of that feather to show you what it represents for you. You may then feel drawn to ask to be adorned with those particular gifts it represents, if appropriate.

The Shaman uses feathers to direct the smoke of smouldering sage they are burning into areas in the home or building that need cleansing, purifying and clearing. It is also a wonderful healing experience to use feathers in this way over the body, as they sweep the aura. We use Cherokee Prayer Fans, which are made with wild turkey feathers, revered and named 'Ground Eagle' by the Cherokee in honour of Thanksgiving. Wet Foot has been crafting these beautiful fans for more than 40 years. The Navajo Prayer Fans, that we use and sell, are crafted by Running Deer. Feathers such as peacock and pheasant come from Tom Gray Elk Rael in Picuris, Pueblo. It is important to note that birds are never ever harmed or killed for their feathers, which are taken (with prayer and ceremony) from naturally fallen stock.

You may find that Spirit gifts you with special feathers. Barbara has a collection of many feathers, that she has been gifted over the years, such as raven, owl, hawk and condor. The Shaman recognises that each type of feather has its own spiritual meaning and significance that can be used in their healing work. Each type of feather can be used to sweep the specific qualities into someone's energy field:

**Hawk:** About guardianship, heightened spirituality, freedom and strength.

**Falcon:** Supports soul healing, speed and movement.

**Goose:** Inspires imagination, potential, loyalty, protection, intuition, bravery, teamwork and fellowship.

**Dove:** Covers love, kindness and peace. A great feather to be used to empower people in love as it's swept over and around the aura.

**Condor:** Relates to visions, independence, sensitivity, leadership, death and rebirth, inspiration and creativity.

**Crow:** Relates to death and rebirth, transition, magic, watchfulness, aids in ability to move between worlds, power and balance of light/dark, straight-talking. This is a great extraction feather.

**Eagle:** Offers great strength, courage, leadership and prestige. The eagle is considered a sacred bird and to receive its feather is a great honour.

**Macaw:** Touches on diplomacy, colour and vibrancy, sharp vision, heightened perception, loyalty, psychic and spiritual development and can bring about emotional and physical healing. Macaw feathers are highly prized and often used in ceremonial costume.

**Owl:** Offers wisdom and the ability to see situations clearly.

**Peacock:** Represents shamanic power, soul flight, journeying, healing and dispelling ignorance or darkness. These birds also represent spiritual and physical purity as well as being omens for good luck.

**Raven:** Magic, rebirth, recovery, renewal, reflection and aids smooth transition. This is a great extraction feather.

**Turkey:** Abundance, pride, connection with Mother Earth, sharing and fertility.

**Swan:** Transformation, grace, balance, purity, beauty, elegance and dream interpretation.

## 13

# Great Spirit

The words 'Wakan Tanka' echoed all around the sweat lodge as Oglala Sioux Ed MacGaa called out to Great Spirit. This was the first time Barbara heard the Lakota meaning for Great Mystery, or Great Spirit. To the Native Americans the Great Spirit is perceived as the Divine power in all things and that which created the Earth. Their belief system holds that all natural objects – rivers, mountains, forests, trees, animals, stones, herbs, plants and birds – have a spirit.

This is a great incomprehensibility for many people who are brought up to believe in only one male god, instead of understanding that the Great Spirit is a beautiful example of a non-theistic belief in an active deity that is intertwined with the life force of the universe.

This appreciation of the Great Spirit, Great Mystery, can only be done through a personal encounter with the living spirits of the land, the elements, the directions and all living creatures.

Today many people are devoid of the Great Mystery while sitting within fabricated buildings with no natural air, fire, earth, pure water or living plants. How can the Great Spirit be heard by someone who has the television blaring while downing numerous cans of lager and with no inspiration around them whatsoever to connect with the great outdoors?

It's time to have a magical experience to become one with all that is...

*Oh Great Spirit: Earth, Sun, Sky and Sea, you are inside; and all around me*
Traditional

# 14

# Healing

The path of the wounded healer, to being whole and healed, is challenging. It is a lifelong process that has continued on from lifetime to lifetime. This process has us going round in cycles, until we finally heal completely from the wounds and injuries we bring with us from our previous lives. Often the same dates, each and every year, bring up particular issues of health. If this sounds familiar then it is a good idea to make a record of each time you are ill, and the symptoms. You may find that colds, sore throats, bad backs and the like occur at the same time every year.

All of us, with nobody excluded, know how it feels to be sad, abandoned, betrayed, lost, fearful and depressed. But it is how we deal with these issues that enables us to learn from the ways of shamanic healing. When we allow ourselves the freedom to explore and observe the teachings of why we are wounded, we can fully integrate with the experience. We can choose whether to learn and understand why an illness is re-occurring or we can abdicate from all responsibility and become the victim.

The problem today in our modern world is that our hospitals and doctors will only fix the physical symptoms. They do not realise the metaphysical symptoms that lie within and cause the physical manifestation of illness and injury. We will not heal until we understand where the illness has manifested from and when we wholly accept the healing itself. In short, nobody else can heal us, except ourselves. Once we are in that place of acceptance we can benefit from the healing of others. It is the combined understanding of the healing of the mind, body, spirit and soul that the Shaman understands. When we look at and understand the mental, emotional, spiritual and physical bodies we are able to focus on reintegration, in order to make ourselves, and others, whole.

The Shaman healer has a deep knowledge of the body and has been through the rites of passage of dismemberment. For they have explored the path of self-knowledge in order to be able to comprehend and understand why and how our wounds occur, and at what level.

The Shaman or shamanic practitioner will traverse the many roads of initiation such as death and rebirth, out-of-body experiences and soul retrieval, to name but a few. By stripping away the original identity of who you are not, made up of others' beliefs and conditioned mentalities, you reveal the soul-flight of the Shaman made whole. This process helps the Shaman have a deep understanding of others' illnesses and woundings. By experience the Shaman has known what it is like to be imbalanced, wounded and confused. Each shamanic healer will have gone through the process of shamanic healing and emerged, like a phoenix from the fire, into a new and deep comprehension of reintegration. Therefore they are no longer the wounded healer, and hold a deep understanding of healing and how to tap into, and heal, the wounds of others.

It is important to understand that before you can heal another, first you must heal yourself, wholly and fully. So many times we have seen people being worked on by healers who are clearly not healed, either in the physical, mental, spiritual or emotional aspects. We have also overheard 'healers' claim to be the next best thing to a holy master. Both of us, combined, have more than 50 years healing experience behind us and we are still learning about how this amazing process works. When you walk through the dark night of the soul, you learn and accept humility and humbleness.

So remember, if you are not feeling well on any level, for example if you have a cold, feel depressed, or have personal problems or worries, then do not offer to heal another person, as you will transfer your energy onto that person.

If we visit our doctor we are usually given 10 or 15 minutes of their time. They have not the time to go deep within and check us on all levels, neither have they purified themselves or the space through cleansing or smudging beforehand, nor prepared mentally by removing their worries and stress. Be aware too that the room also holds the energy of all the illness and fears of every patient who has gone before you. How often have you come out of the doctor's surgery feeling worse than when you went in?

There are many ways in which one can work with shamanic healing. Firstly, the most important aspect before working on anyone is to have an understanding of biology, psychology and physiology. A Shaman healer must be able to connect with their spirit guides and guardians, and have a complete comprehension of the working of soul retrieval, extraction and removal of attachments.

As Shamans we use our intuition, our experience, our learned knowledge, our inner knowing, our wisdom and feelings to help, heal and guide those through the shamanic healing process. At no time can we as practitioners take our personal issues and negative energies into a healing session with our clients. This would be potential damaging and very irresponsible.

Take the time to prepare yourself for facilitating a shamanic healing. Have a shower, put on clean, loose clothing. Prepare your room, by space clearing with sage, burning incense or herbs. Light candles and place your tools, such as your drum and feathers, on your altar. Create a warm, loving, nurturing space that your client will feel special, safe and secure in. Before your client arrives sit down and connect with your spirit guardians, gate keepers, ancestors or loved ones in the spirit world who will help and assist you. Call on your power animals to help you in any soul retrieval or extraction work.

When you are ready, welcome your client into your sacred space. Make them feel at ease. Play soft music in the background and offer them a glass of water. When they are ready, begin with asking how you can help them. Let them talk, as you listen well. While they are talking, use your visionary skills to track into their past lives, this life and future lifetimes. You are seeking and searching for the original wounding, the root cause of disease. Then, when the client has finished sharing the relevant information, you can perform the shamanic healing method that is suitable.

Every Shaman or shamanic practitioner has various tools for working with shamanic healing. The focus point is not to use your hands, unless you really wish to. Shamanic healing in its very essence is not to use your hands, but to heal and extract with your tools. Why would anyone wish to take it upon themselves to collect another's disease or illness through their physical body?

When you are ready, begin by trusting in the guidance of Spirit to work through you, in order to help and assist your client to the best of your abilities. Trust what information you are given and notice any change in your client's wellbeing. It is important to advise your client that they should always consult a doctor when they are ill. Do not make a diagnosis, unless you are a qualified doctor, nurse or physician.

Once you have finished the shamanic healing, assist the client gently to a seated position, if they have been lying down, and offer them a glass of water. This will help to ground them. When they are ready ask them how they feel and what they experienced through the process. It is so important to be a good listener and observe, for this will help you greatly in your work as a shamanic healer. Every healing session teaches us more about the work we do.

When you have finished your session, thank them for coming and wish them well. We always let our clients know that we are available as support and welcome feedback on their progress. You can carry on your work by visiting them in the dreamtime, with their permission of course.

Below is a list of tools that you can work with in shamanic

healing. It is important to note that healing techniques vary from Shaman to Shaman. Always follow your intuition and your guides when performing shamanic healing. Trust what you are getting and always put your client's comfort and safety first. There are many good shamanic practitioner courses out there that teach the many healing methods of the Shaman. Again, use your intuition and inner knowing in order to pick the right one for you. You may wish to check the back of this book for details on our Walking the Sacred Wheel, Shamanic Studies course.

**Shamanic Tools**
**Bells**: Sound healing
**Bones**: Vibrational healing and extraction
**Crystals**: Vibrational healing and extraction
**Didgeridoo**: Sound healing and extraction
**Drums**: Sound healing and extraction
**Feathers**: Smudging and extraction
**Flutes**: Sound healing and extraction
**Gongs**: Sound healing
**Rattles**: Sound healing and extraction
**Sage**: Smudging and purifying
**Stones**: Vibrational healing and extraction
**Voice/Chants**: Sound healing

Then there is the significant matter of healing the original wounding. Deep within each and every one of us lies our soul's original wounding. This wounding carries fears, pains, and despairs from all our previous lifetimes, not only of ourselves, but also from all the people who have been in our lives. Remember that their fears, beliefs and faiths have played a big part in creating who we are *not*. It is by practicing the art of discernment that we can separate their thoughts and actions from our own. By uncovering and revealing this wounding we heal and recover all the fragmented pieces of our soul, thus becoming whole and complete once more.

From lifetime to lifetime we carry forward all our cellular memories to help and assist us in the next lifetime. Unfortunately not all those memories are good ones. Those pains and fears that are not explainable in this lifetime can only have come from past lives and past memories. These trapped emotions and memories reside not only within our DNA, but also in the body's muscular network. After an accident or incident the Shaman, who understands this process, looks for the reason and goes deep within to see if something similar has happened before in another lifetime. An accident will trigger the cellular memory from deep with our subconscious. It then activates a fear response or pain stimuli and the situation, in our mind, gets out of control. Our minds can escalate these negative thoughts to a point where it affects our day-to-day living. What needs to be discerned is whether the intense reaction stems from this lifetime or whether it is a trigger from our original wounding, replaying over and over again. It is just like a record that gets stuck in time and space.

If our emotions and feeling are running amok then we end up totally confused and out of control. We need to understand that our emotions play a very important part in our daily lives. By honouring and listening to our feelings and emotions, and defining them from the monkey chatter mind that leads us astray, we can start to heal. This is when we start to trust instead of dismissing our true knowing.

Today our hospitals are full to breaking point and for many of the patients their admission is a cry for help. Most people in the hospital are not there because of physical ailments, but because their spirits are crushed, their souls fragmented, their emotions drained or restrained and their minds confused, manifested in the physical through illness or accidents. The law of attraction runs deep!

When Barbara's dad had a heart attack she asked the sister of the heart ward he was in if she could question the other male patients about their lives. What she discovered was very inter-esting. Of the 32 men who had suffered a heart attack, 22 of them had recently lost their wives through death or divorce. This is a clear case of heartache on an emotional level. Six of the remaining 10 men were overweight and were literally eating themselves to death because they had no love, felt isolated or rejected, or had mental and emotional issues. The other four were there because they were homeless and did not feel supported in a spiritual or physical way by the system and society. Of course, none of the patients, nor the hospital staff, would be consciously aware of this.

What was very clear was that in this heart ward the problems were caused by instability of not being supported through life's traumas. Instead of the doctors looking at the medical condition as a whole (of mind, body, sprit and soul combined) they only look at the body and not what is causing the underlying problem.

However, a medicine man or woman, or Shaman, will look at the whole. They will look into your original wounding, your past lives, connect with the spirits, look at this lifetime and tap into your destiny. This form of healing, or doctoring, is the only way that in today's society we can hope to heal the masses of people who are queuing for hospital appointments. We need to pinpoint and heal the underlying original wounding that has brought about the accident, illness or disease. We can do this through the diversity of using various healing tools such as psychology for the mind, complementary therapies for the body, retrieving fragmented parts of the soul coupled with extraction work, and a good ear for listening to what the patient is really saying.

For thousands of years the art of soul retrieval has been healing people in many cultures all around the world. This ancient shamanic practice has helped heal many illnesses caused by soul loss. It is important to understand that if the soul is ill then the whole body is out of balance. The soul is the principle of life for each individual. Unfortunately today not many people even know that they have a soul. In ancient times the healers and Shamans knew that soul loss was attributed to the soul being stolen, or frightened away. Today parts of the soul often depart when a loved one dies, through surgery, comas, during sexual abuse including incest and the misuse of drugs or alcohol.

Fragments are often lost when people give away their personal power, having been verbally or psychically attacked. Often putting others before our own needs, a lack of self worth and losing one's inner child due to premature responsibility will result in fragmentation, as well as stress and distress. Of course, the person does not realise what is happening, but all of the above are likely to cause a soul part to depart to a more loving and nurturing environment.

Soul retrieval is part of a process that can heal original wounding and soul loss. The shamanic practitioner journeys to the Lower World or Upper World where the fragmented parts reside. This cannot be accessed without the help and assistance of your power animals, allies and spirit helpers. By bringing these missing parts of the soul back and reconnecting them to the person, they will once again feel whole and complete. This action restores harmony and personal power, helping them to be balanced on a mental, physical and emotional level and therefore igniting the spirit within.

So, how do you know if you are suffering from soul loss? You will feel stuck, lost and unable to move on in your current situation. You might feel abandoned or betrayed by others. You are not able to let go of the past or the hurts you have suffered from others. You may feel powerless and not able to control or change your life. You could feel numb, have a lack of emotions or feelings, and you might even hate yourself for reasons you don't understand.

If you feel you need help with original wounding or soul loss, seek out a good shamanic practitioner or Shaman in your area.

There are also some good books on the subject. For those of you wishing to learn more about these techniques please see the back of the book for information on our shamanic home studies course, available online.

Many people do not realise that their illnesses can be caused by spiritual intrusion. This is usually a malevolent spirit that has slipped in through the person's misuse of drugs, alcohol, using a Ouija board or dabbling in the occult with no experience or protection in place. Another way that a spiritual intrusion can occur is if angry, bitter, jealous or evil thoughts are directed at you from another person. These negative thought-forms can cause a lot of damage to the person on the receiving end, who is being psychically attacked.

Another way you might suffer an intrusion is by self-harm. This doesn't have to be deliberately done through physically abusing yourself. It can happen without even realising that you are harming yourself. If your thoughts are predominately about sickness and symptoms, you create and affirm that illness though your own thought process. This attracts malevolent spirits through your own creation of negative thought-forms, who will feeds off the energy. The Shaman will work with this misplaced energy within the body by performing an 'extraction'. In today's society 'energy' is not understood, and all too often dismissed. It's not surprising how many people claim to feel 'different', not like themselves anymore, after having an organ transplant. Of course, to the Shaman it is obvious, for that organ holds and retains cellular memory of the body and soul of the person it was originally designed for. Extraction work will draw out the energy, freeing the patient up to enjoy newfound freedom and health on all levels.

If you find you need a shamanic extraction then seek an experienced Shaman or shaman practitioner to assist you. They will use their shamanic tools to extract and transmute the misplaced energy into positive energy, either by burying it in the earth, placing it in water, or cleansing it with fire. The Shaman will journey to a shamanic state of consciousness, calling on their power animals and spirit guides to help and assist them in the removal of the intrusions. It is very important that at no time does a Shaman extract the intrusion into their own body. Once the extraction is done the Shaman will fill the void with pure healing energy.

You can also remove your own intrusions or misplaced energy by visualisation. Imagine swimming in a lake, or lying out in the sun to fill your body with sunlight. Drink prayed-over water and see, in your mind's eye, misplaced energy being washed away. You could do the same in the shower as you feel and imagine the water cleansing and healing you.

# Herbs

The ancients used herbs and incenses for clearing, cleansing and sacred ceremony. Among the herbs primarily used was, and still is today in many cultures, the wild garden herb *salvia officinalis*, meaning 'to be saved'. Today, we call it sage. It originated on the island of Crete. In ancient times it was used to protect against evil, for curing snakebites and increasing women's fertility.

Theophrastus (a student of Plato) wrote about two different sages, one being an under shrub that he called *sphakos* and a similar plant that he named *elelisphakos*, which was later called *salvia* by the Romans. They used *salvia* as a diuretic and a local anaesthetic. In modern excavations at the Temple of Karnak, in Luxor, Egypt, fragments of sage were found in the ruins of the huge baths built there during the Roman occupation. The sage was used in the hot steaming waters to relieve aching muscles and sore feet. For thousands of years sage has been recognised for its healing properties and purification abilities and was used by many ancient cultures throughout the world.

It was cultivated in monastery gardens and popular in kitchens during the Middle Ages, being acknowledged for its healing properties and value in those days too. Recognising the miraculous attributes of sage, another name for it was *salvia salvatrix*, meaning 'sage the saviour'. It was used, among other herbs, to ward off plagues. The Ancient Greeks extolled the virtues of sage and associated it with immortality, longevity and increasing mental capacity. There is modern evidence that sage can effectively help manage moderate forms of Alzheimer's disease. In Britain sage has been listed as one of the most important culinary herbs for generations. Today it appears along with onion in the form of stuffing, as an accompaniment to roast poultry dishes.

Sage has been highly revered as a sacred plant throughout the ages and folklore says that if you write your wishes onto a sage leaf and pop it under your pillow, your dreams will come true. Today there are more than 500 varieties of sage that are cultivated or naturally grow in the world. Before using sage as a culinary, spiritual, cultural or medicinal herb, you will need to make sure you have chosen the right type. For rituals, ceremony, cleansing, purification and protection we personally use the Californian white sage, 'salvia apiana', which is what we will be focusing on through these pages.

Flavia's first experience with sage was in ceremony in Hawaii. As she stepped into the sacred space she was surrounded by the smouldering smoke of burning sage by a respected Shaman. Surprised by its immediate effects she felt fully cleansed and light, enabling her to become the clearest channel for Spirit that she had encountered up to that time. Flavia has an awesome respect for the herb and continues to use it daily, for herself and for others, in her workshops across the UK.

Barbara's first encounter with sage was a surprisingly emotional one for her. It was 30 years ago that she was invited to her first sweat lodge, near Arizona in New Mexico. As she stepped inside the purpose-built lodge, for ceremony and purification, she noticed that the entire ground was covered in sacred sage. The overwhelming aroma hit her and she broke down in tears. She recalls this as the hottest lodge she has ever experienced and that during the ceremony she became increasingly distressed, wanting to run out into the cool night air. But it was Grandfather Sage who gently nurtured her, calling with his scent through the darkness and humidity, encouraging her to endure the process through to the end. Within the comfort of the sage she sobbed and sobbed throughout the ceremony as she was able to release many unwanted fears and traumas that had dogged her for years. The sage had set her free.

Over the years since that time sage has played a very big part in her life. Seeing sage as an old and trusted friend she has honoured it by wearing a hand-made crown of the sacred herb during her ceremonial Sun Dance years with the Lakota, and continues to use it daily for protection and purification for herself and for others in her work as a Shaman.

The Californian white sage that we use and sell is wild crafted by a Elliot, a wonderful man who gathers and bundles the sacred herb from the Californian land. His work is dedicated to sage and he has built a respect for the sage, which in turn is reciprocated.

He says: 'Gathering sage and making sage bundles is a prayer and meditation for me. Each of my bundles carries prayers from my heart to yours. I strongly believe in the healing and purifying powers of sage and hope my smudge sticks bring you blessings too.'

Elliot gathers his sage in late spring and summer, when the leaves are in full bloom. He makes sure that he only collects from the bushes that are heavily foliaged, so that no plant becomes sparse. He always asks permission from the ancestors of the land, the animals that may benefit from the sage or area, and from the plants themselves, making sure that he has full permission before he gathers. Time is also important to him and is mindful of the cycles of the moon, trying to collect the leaves during the phase of the full moon, so that the bushes are drenched in the magical properties of its light. After harvesting he sweeps round the area to check he has not left anything behind and gives an act of thanks by leaving an offering. This is the shamanic way, working with nature, the land and the spirits.

**Smudge Stick:** This is a bundle of sage bound together with string, made into a cigar-like shape. Our best-selling size is the four inch mini, which is perfect for travelling and self-smudging. The other popular sizes are the medium bundle, eight inches, and the large, which is ten inches.

**Loose Leaf Sage:** This is small individual pieces of sage sold in a clear bag, the equivalent of two small sage sticks. It is perfect for using small quantities at any given time.

**Sage Spray:** This is made of a blend of Californian white sage essential oil, gem crystal water and pure spring water, with alcohol used as a preservative, as in all essences. It is ideal for clearing auras, cleansing a treatment room, as a purifying perfume and for use in any location where one is unable to actually burn sage.

We use sage today for the same reasons it has always been in use – smudging and purification. Tribal people knew the protective properties of this sacred herb and used it to clear the energy and auric fields of people, homes, rocks and plants, which all take on our own and others' negative energy. It is so important to clear and cleanse any unwanted energies, particularly in this day and age, as it tends to be ignored. When we hold onto old energies (situations, conversations or negative occurrences of the past) and other people's negativities, we become diseased and out of alignment. We have seemed to have lost the ancient art of purifi-cation, which was – and still should be – a daily ritual. Fortunately these sacred herbs are still here today, offering their assistance to work with us in that way.

### Smudging Your Aura

Take the sage, hold it and connect with the spirit of the sage you have in your hands and state your intention – this could be to cleanse your energy field, to protect yourself or heal. Smudging brings a sense of wellbeing, and in our many workshops where we smudge, a participant always says afterwards, without fail, that they feel cleansed, clear and so much lighter. Once you have made your connection with your sage medicine teacher, take your shell and hold it in the palm of your hand or, place it on your altar, table or put it on the ground. If you are using a sage stick you may wish to pull parts of the leaves from it and place it in the shell or simply light the end of the whole stick. Light the sage, making sure the flame goes out and then let the sage smoulder. It is this you are working with, not the flame. To cleanse yourself use your hands to sweep the smoke up and around your body, or if you have been gifted a feather, use it for this very purpose and sweep the body and auric field. The smoke from an incense stick or the spray can also be used around your aura to smudge yourself. Note: there is no right or wrong way in smudging yourself or others, it is about intention. Let the spirit of the sage guide you, as in all sacred practices throughout the ages.

## Smudging Others

If you are asked to smudge another person, or animal, you will need to have a working knowledge of how the body works on an energetic level. Again, choose the type of sage you'd like to burn in the shell, such as loose or whole stick. Make your intentions, as above. When working with others we strongly recommend using a feather to direct the sage smoke to all areas of their body, paying particular attention to places that look, in your mind's eye, or feel in need of healing or energetic replenishing. Sweep the feather up and around the aura as well as using it on the body to pull down and off unwanted energies. Ask the person to hold out their arms, make sure you cover front and back, from the top of the head down to the soles of their feet. See this as a very important spiritual shower, cleansing every part of their energy. Traditionally we always work sunwise (clockwise), but again what feels right for one, may not feel right for another, so go with your intuition. When you have finished, use your feather to check that there are no heavy energies left on or around the person/animal. Stand in front of them and direct some final sage around them before finishing at the heart centre. It is nice then to finish with a prayer of dedication for their wellbeing.

## Smudging Rooms and Sacred Spaces

If you are doing any therapeutic, complementary therapy work it is so important to always cleanse your room before you work, and importantly between each client. This will cleanse the room of any energies that have been left behind by the client and the work performed on them. Likewise do this when moving into a new home, workplace or hotel room.

We are on the road most of the year and if we stay in a hotel we always spritz the room first with some handy handbag/pocket sized sage spray. This cleanses the room and eliminates any energies of the previous occupant. Sage spray is so convenient to use for a quick fix and when it is impossible to light sage. The work place is a prime example. If you need to cleanse yourself from others' energies after a meeting or phone call or just clean the general office environment, spray a mist around you discreetly and you will feel much clearer and lighter. The same goes for any similar encounter with family and friends, after meeting with them, chatting on the phone or a house visit.

We do the same before each of our workshops and talks to clear the room and to bring in the positive healing energies of sage for our audience members. We tend to burn or spray sage at our stand we have at the Mind, Body, Spirit shows we present at, around the UK and beyond. This protects us from all the combined energies of the people who visit, as well as clearing the space to bring in blessings and prosperity. We love sage!

So simply sweep with your feather, or allow 'solo' smoking sage to cleanse all areas of space, by starting at the door and taking it in a sunwise direction in its shell to the four corners of the room (corners are where energies tend to stick – which is why our ancestors lived in round houses by the way!) and then finish at the door. You can then simply let the sage smoulder in the shell on a table, or from chosen part of the room if you wish. A burning sage incense stick or sage spray will work just as well, with the best of intentions.

## Smudging Crystals and Tools

There are many different ways to clear and cleanse the spiritual tools you may use in your work. For example, many crystal healers cleanse their stones in water and lay them out in the moonlight to recharge their energy. This is a wonderful method and by all means continue this practice if you use it. However, it is good to know that you can smudge your crystals with sage to clear and cleanse them, making this a popular, quick and easy method when necessary. Likewise, you can smudge with sage to clear and cleanse any other tools such as shamanic drums, rattles, statues, tarot or oracle cards or anything else that you work with. This is necessary to do, especially if someone else has handled your sacred objects as you will need to rid that person's energies. You can do this by the same method as clearing a room. Pass the smouldering sage in its shell, and perhaps using a feather to direct it over your altar, or wherever you keep your sacred items, to clear the energy. You can also pass any of your tools or objects through the smoke to cleanse them that way.

## Burning and Extinguishing Your Sage

If you find the sage burning profusely, even if only a little is lit, remember it has a life of its own. If there is no breeze or winds, then this is a sign from the sage that more is to be used and burned for the job in hand. If you find it difficult to light your sage stick (you may find that the end has blackened) then unwind the cotton that the stick has been bound in, and then use individual leaves taken from the stick. Barbara has seen so many sage sticks left and abandoned over the years, due to lighting difficulties, because of people not realising that the cotton can be taken off. The cotton is for packaging purposes only to hold the sage together. So feel free to unravel the cotton when lighting and using your sage stick. To extinguish the sage, place it into a vessel filled with sand or soil and stub it out into it. This is why we mentioned earlier that you should collect soil from a favourite place in nature to use in your shell.

## Storing Your Sage

When not in use, store your sage in a cool dry place such as a Tupperware box, glass jar, or paper bag to keep the freshness and live energy of the sage. We always put all our sage back in their boxes after a show or event. You can pop a stick into clothes drawers or wardrobes to make the most of its scent, if you wish, or keep a stick on your altar for handy usage.

## When Not To Use Sage

It is advisable not to use sage when you are pregnant as it can be prone to lead to miscarriage if your body is not used to it, as with any herb. Nor should a pregnant lady inhale the smoke of lit sage.

### Elemental Prayer Ritual

You will need the following:

**Sage:** Represents the element of Earth.
**Shell:** Represents the element of Water.
**Lighter, Fire or Candle Flame:** Represents the element of Fire.
**Smoke from Lit Sage:** Represents the element of Air.
**Prayers:** Represent the element of Spirit.

Set your intentions and prayers. Visualise yourself sitting in a five pointed star, the Pentagram, protecting and linking you to the five elements of Earth, Water, Fire, Air and Spirit.

Put the lit sage in the shell and as the smoke rises upwards visualise the Pentagram spiralling up and spinning around you, fully covering and protecting you. Start chanting or speaking the following words as this happens: *'Earth of my body, heal me. Water of my blood, cleanse me. Air of my breath, purify me. Fire of my spirit, ignite me. Spirit of my prayers, teach me.'*

Now offer your prayers as the sage smoke rises and takes

them up to Great Spirit. Once finished chant five times to the elements and spirits: *'Guard me, protect me, encircle me, empower me, free me.'*

When you feel fully protected give your thanks and extinguish your sage safely, and place it back in your storage space, or on your altar.

## Ceremonies for Healing

### Personal Healing Ceremony

Set your intentions and light sage in your shell or vessel. Once smouldering, sit with it in front of you and gently breathe in the aroma and draw the essence of the sage into your body, directing it to areas in need of healing.

Alternatively take some unlit sage and place it onto the part of your body that requires healing. Call upon the spirit of the sage to bring about healing and comfort to that area.

### Healing Another Person

When working on healing someone else, light a small sage stick and then blow onto it, causing the smoke to enter into the area you are treating.

To work in ceremony with sage just let the spirit of the sage lead you and then follow your intuition. You can't go wrong. Remember it is all about intention while drawing on the sacred and healing properties of this herb. When Barbara injured herself in the Badlands of South Dakota she instinctively grabbed a handful of sage and applied it to her wound, which stopped bleeding immediately, leading to a perfect healing.

### Sage Tea

Sage tea has been taken to cure ailments such as colds and sore throats and is still favoured by the Chinese to this day. As a medicinal herb, the forms it is most used in are infusions, extracts, oils, tinctures and poultices.

Make sage tea by placing a handful of fresh sage leaves into a teapot and pouring over that a pint of water that has boiled, but allow it to cool for a short while before pouring. Cover this and steep for about ten minutes and then strain it into a cup. Sage tea is wonderful taken with honey, lemon or sugar. Store cold tea for a mouthwash to gargle away sore throats or bad breath.

Note: it is really important when buying sage to ask where it has been hand crafted and by whom. There are many bundles being sold out there which have sage mixed with other herbs, such as sweet grass, lavender, pine, juniper and copal.

One of the first lessons in shamanic practice is, 'Do not mix your medicines!' What we mean by this is, be careful not to blend the different properties that are provided by individual plant types, unless of course you are an experienced herbalist and understand the mix of those properties.

## Sweetgrass (Hierochloe Odorata)

Sweetgrass hails from Montana, Wyoming and the Dakotas in the US. It is harvested when it reaches about 14 inches in height and then is traditionally braided to represent the hair braids of the grandmothers of Mother Earth. Sweetgrass is a great purifier and is used to bring in positive energy. It is therefore great to call in and burn on charcoal discs after sage has been used. Sweetgrass is placed on the Grandfathers (heated rocks) in the sweat lodge.

## Cedar (Juniperus Virginia)

We use red cedar for cleansing, clearing and purification. Like the sweetgrass it should be burnt on a charcoal disc. Cedar is known to bring in good influences and is the main purification herb used at the Lakota Sun Dance rituals.

## Palo Santo Wood (Holy Wood)

Palo Santo is a mystical tree that grows on the coast of South America and is related to myrrh, frankincense and copal. Its properties are similar to sage. Shamans and medicine people burn it for cleansing and purification. Use a candle flame, match or lighter holding it at a 45 degree angle while pointing the tip of the wood down to the flame. Allow it to burn for around 30 seconds to a minute and then blow the flame out, allowing the wood to smoulder. Use it as you would sage, to clear, cleanse and purify. Barbara first experienced Palo Santo during an ayahuasca ceremony in the Amazon. It created the most amazing smell that supported her through the ritual, due to its healing energies.

*Disclaimer: these statements are not intended to diagnose or cure or prevent any disease.*

# 16

# Incense Sticks

Incense sticks are a convenient way to clear and cleanse and there are variety of sage incense sticks on the market today. Be careful not to choose those with carcinogenic ingredients, of which many popular brands are made. It is so important to be aware of this. Always check the ingredients because you do not want to be breathing in poisons while meditating and connecting with Spirit!

We use the pure unadulterated incense sticks made by Fred Soll. These are natural and are made from pure resin, essential oils and herbs. The incense stick is hand dipped into the resin and oil, sprinkled with sage herbs and then laid out to dry in the New Mexico sun. We have visited Fred Soll in New Mexico and watched a part of this very dedicated process, which takes up to three weeks!

# 17

# Journeying

For most shamanic practitioners and Shamans, the shamanic journey with drums, rattles and bells is the first method used to access the Lower World and Upper World to seek guidance from the ancestors and spirits. Each Shaman will have techniques and skills, that will vary from Shaman to Shaman, that enable them to reach the other worlds. This is just like separate people driving to a venue but taking alternate routes still gets them to the same destination. Everyone journeying will have different experiences and stories to tell. It is important to know that there is no wrong or right way to journey. You will be guided by your power animals or allies who will advise you on the many roads you will travel.

Often people won't journey because of a deep fear of getting lost, or not being able to come back from the journey. There is also a deep seated belief for many, often passed on by family or religion, that it is wrong to practice shamanism, that it's dangerous and frightening. There are those who fear to journey because they like to be in control. The last thing these people want to do is allow themselves to drop down, let go of all their fears and discomforts and discover first hand for themselves where their power lies.

However, with journeying comes many advantages for your health and wellbeing. Sitting with a drum and beating it constantly with a one beat over a period of, say, ten minutes, will help you to stop thinking, to silence the monkey chatter mind. You will find that after doing this short journeying you will feel revitalized.

The vibration of the drum will soothe you, calm you and make you feel good. Sometimes when people use the drum for the first time it is very overwhelming. Memories often come flooding back of previous life times. Visions will flash in front of you and so you will know that you have started on a journey to revisit and remember what you once knew.

You will have taken a journeying from ordinary everyday awareness, with all its behavioural patterns of fear, control, others' belief systems and cultural conditioning, into a world of non-ordinary awareness and viewpoints that are detached. This spiritual perspective is not easily obtainable in the Middle World of selves. From this deep place of contemplation you now go inwards to receive the answer you have been searching for. The shamanic journey is undertaken for purposes of personal healing or healing of others, to meet your power animal or spirit guide or for divination. Your personal soul flight is life-changing when you discover these inner realms.

These archetypal worlds bequeathed to us from our ancient ancestors reside in the collective unconsciousness, a part of the matrix woven as a rich tapestry of life for all to see, if you indeed embark upon the journey. When you take your first journey you will see many things. You may travel up and down the Cosmic Tree from the Upper World to the Lower World. Colours, shapes and sound will appear different as you travel along the river of forgetfulness that conceals your past thoughts, feelings and missing parts of your soul. This is the journey of your soul's flight to come to visit and drink of the knowledge and wisdom that has been hidden for too long from you by others.

Now let's begin a journey with the drum. If you don't have your own drum then we suggest you get a CD of shamanic drumming (see the back of this book for details of how to purchase one). Make sure you are somewhere safe and quiet where you will not be disturbed. If you are listening to a drumming CD you may wish to lie down. Place a blindfold or some material across your eyes so that you are in total darkness. Switch on the recording and just relax. Have no preconceived ideas. Relax. If any thoughts come up just let them go. The more you listen to the recording the more your mind will be in silence and not chatter. Allow yourself to journey on the sound and the vibration, which carries you from world to world, reality to reality.

Those of you who have a drum (again, to purchase one see the back of this book) we would suggest that you sit with your drum and make a connection with it first of all. Sit with your hand placed on the centre of the drum skin. Ask the spirit of the drum to help and assist you in your journey to the other worlds. When you are ready, take time out in a quiet place, or even better in a wood or grove where nobody is around. With your back leaning up against your favourite tree, make the connection with the Cosmic Tree. If you are at home then find a comfortable chair, or sit on the floor with your drum. Make sure nobody will disturb you. Let the journey begin by allowing the drum to drum you. As the mundane world disappears you will find yourself journeying. Be the observer and observe everything around you, who you meet and what you see. Enjoy, let go and allow your imagination to be the portal to the world of spirit.

Once you stop drumming, or when the CD is finished, write down your experiences in your shamanic journal book. Your journey might not make sense to you at first. However, as you continue to make your soul flights you will find yourself able to travel to the Lower World and Upper World by your focus and visualisation. Soon you will find yourself travelling down through tree trunks and caves entrances into the Lower World or you may find yourself journeying upwards in a spiral of white light or riding on the winds. Every journey is different, no two are ever the same. Once you have used the drum or recording, try using different tools for the journey. Maybe use a rattle, or a CD with a repetitive chant or sound. Journey once again to the Shaman's universe and enjoy the ride!

## 18

# Medicine Bags

Barbara was always collecting stones, shells and feathers from a very early age. She would gather them in a bundle and wrap them in cloth or materials that she loved. She often wore feathers in her hair and witches' stones round her neck and carried her special stones in a shoulder bag until it became too full and heavy. Eventually her room was overfilled with all that she had collected from visiting sacred sites, lakes, shorelines and beaches. When she began travelling the world, as an adult, she visited a shop in Santa Fe and noticed small leather bags hanging from the counter. The owner, Mary, explained that these were medicine bags that she had crafted for those who are called to walk the medicine way. Coins, bones and crystals from all over the world adorned the bags. As Barbara looked at them it brought back all the memories of where she had travelled. Mary handed her one of the medicine bags as a gift. As soon as its strap was placed around her neck the whole room spun. She saw a vision of all the places that the artefacts had come from to make this sacred medicine bag. As soon as she got home she placed within it the most sacred of her crystals, a hummingbird feather, her first sage from her first sweat lodge, her first charcoal from her fire keeper days and a stone from the top of Machu Picchu.

A man was found frozen high in a mountain range in the USA, who had died 5,000 years ago. He was wearing a medicine bag around his neck containing medicinal plants, a net similar to a dream catcher and a copper headed axe.

A Shaman's medicine bag is worn around the neck as protection both for the front and back of the body in order to protect you both from the past, of what lies behind, and the future, of what lies in front. Placed over the heart centre, it contains stones, herbs such as sage, bones, hair and fur, feathers, shells and many other small sacred objects. The medicine bag is carried by Shamans to maintain personal right relationships with the world around them. Carrying personal objects enables the Shaman to connect with and be a part of the sacred. The purpose of this sacred medicine is to make contact with the natural spiritual forces that surround them. This supernatural power is carried by the medicine man or woman, or Shaman, and is for their eyes only. Upon their death they are buried with it.

The bags are usually made of leather or cloth. In our Celtic tradition we call them crone bags or Druidic crane bags, which are used for protection and good luck. Another name for a medicine bag is a spirit medicine bag. Again this is an empowerment tool and carries within it personal items meaning a lot to a person, such as a ring or a picture of a loved one.

## 19

# Medicine Bundles

The sacred contents of a Native American medicine bundle are considered holy by the tribe, clan or community, or the individual who keeps the medicine of the community safe. It must never touch the ground. The contents are kept secret, known only to the 'carriers' who hold a sacred responsibility to all the people concerned in the community. The ceremonies and rituals associated with the medicine bundles are handed down from generation to generation. Women are the keepers of the sacred bundles and are regarded as holy. The sacred bundles that the Aztecs and Quiche Mayans owned carried mystical powers.

Today many shamanic practitioners own medicine bundles that they have collected during their travels and journeys from around the world. Our bundles hold all the memories and tools used in our various journeys and work in different parts of the world, from vision quests, to Sun Dance, to sweat lodges and visits to ancient sacred sites. To connect fully to those places and moments, we hold the bundle to our foreheads, or hearts, and welcome the visions of those sacred times in sacred ceremony. If you are called to make a medicine bag or bundle, go on a vision quest to first find out your personal medicine, your power animals and your true purpose and calling. This is a sacred bond between you and spirit. Take your time to collect your personal power just as the native people do. This is your medicine, your teachings. Then go and collect all that is sacred to you, which awaits you across the four corners of this beautiful planet.

# Medicine Names

Tribal cultures from around the world have many different ways of welcoming their newborn onto the Earth. They recognise that these children hold the essence of spirit, and with them bring great wisdom and understanding direct from the Summerlands. The newborn souls still have a direct link with Creator and therefore remember who they are and where they have come from. Sometimes some of these will even remember their names from previous lifetimes. All through Flavia's childhood she often referred to herself as Maria. This was a remembrance of a previous lifetime, with which she has linked further through shamanic journeying and past-life connection.

In certain traditions and tribes, before being gifted with their name, the child is observed over a period of time to see what the child is drawn to. In many cultures the baby's name represents many aspects of nature, a god or goddess name, mystical entities, saints or other names from holy books or perhaps the parents' favourite pop star, such as Elvis or Madonna. The names given in the Hindu tradition are very important and the way this is done involves looking at the child's horoscope to determine the date and time of birth, the birth star, the forefather's name and the deities linked to that time of birth. In African villages children are first given a name that is later changed when they reach the time for their rite of passage, called puberty or coming of age. Some of the tribal customs call upon the local Shaman or medicine man or woman to cast the bones to see the destiny of the child who is about to be born.

It is so important to understand the meaning of your given name. All souls know exactly what name they would like to be called by and impart that knowledge to the parents to be. Often the parents hear, subconsciously of course, and name the child correctly. But do they understand the meaning of that name, and does the child, once they come onto the Earth plane of existence? Sadly not all parents hear, and name the child something totally unsuitable to the child itself and to their life path. Our names are clues to who we are and what we are here to do.

Before her adoption, Barbara was named Morag. This was subsequently changed when her adoptive parents took her in as Barbara Margaret. At 13 years old she was given her pagan name of 'Raven' by Swein MacDonald the Highland Seer, named because of her natural connection with these birds when she was out in nature. As an adult Barbara spent time in the American Native lands where she was gifted her medicine name of 'Morning Star Hawk Woman'. It took her many years to become her name and it was only when she had completed 11 years of Sun Dance did she use it.

Flavia's name means golden or yellow haired and is an old Roman family name. Flavia was born naturally blonde, which fitted her name perfectly. However, right from the start Flavia recognised her past life links with Rome and Pompeii and under-stood that her name was given as a reminder as to who she was and had been. Despite memories of other past lives and names, she knew that the Roman incarnation must have some connection with the work she has come to do in this lifetime. Like Barbara, Flavia's natural infinity with nature, and her work as a child with rooks, provided her with her pagan name, Rook. In later adulthood Flavia was led to change her hair from blonde to red (as part of a fire initiation – see the Power Animals section in this book for the full story) and finally her long awaited medicine name of 'Red Spirit Woman' was gifted to her by Oglala Sioux Ed McGaa Eagle Man upon their first meeting.

Many people go to a Shaman or medicine man or woman to receive their medicine or spirit name. Once the request has been made and a gift exchanged they will take time to ask the spirits to assist them in finding name. Once found, the Shaman or elder will get in touch to confirm the name they've been called.

It may, however, be suggested that you go on a vision quest to connect with the spirits and to ask them to reveal your name to you. You might go to a sweat lodge and be invited to ask for your spirit name, as Edd McGaa does in his lodge naming ceremonies. This is a very powerful way to receive your name. If you are not happy with the name you are gifted, if it is not to your liking, it will be what is needed for you at the time. Go within to understand what it is that makes you feel uncomfortable. This in itself is a great teacher of strength and understanding. Once you have your name, sit with it and find out all you can about it. In time you will become your name through experience and walking the medicine way.

Our names hold great meaning and it is time for you, if you are reading this book, to ask yourself, 'Does my name hold my medicine?' Do you know what your medicine is? If not, how can you become it? By becoming your medicine you are in effect changing your way of life. A spiritual name is a vibration that helps to elevate your personal power and energy through the meaning of the name. Your spirit name or medicine name is your soul's identity. By connecting with your new name you start to focus on your highest potential. Making the choice to receive and become your new name is taking a step towards leaving old habits and patterns behind you and connecting with the new you. You become what you create through sound and vibration. By creating a new name you are in effect rebirthing yourself.

Look at all the celebrities who have changed their names before they became famous; Elton John was Reginald Kenneth Dwight, Marilyn Monroe was Norma Jean Mortenson, to name but two. If they had not changed their names would they still have become famous? We remember people by their names, for names have a deliberate and unique signature resonance sound to them. Universally a name tells all of who a person is. It is said that a leprechaun will not reveal his name for that very reason! Try sounding or chanting your name. How does it sound? Does it sound good, do you feel comfortable with it? If not, then question why and then change it.

Yes, you can change you name if you wish to. You have a choice. You are not stuck with the name you were given if you don't like it. You don't have to live with your name and you might find that when you do change your name by deed poll, like thousands of others, your life will change. Egyptian pharaohs were changing their names all the time to suit the situations that presented themselves, such as battles, births, marriages and many other festivities and ceremonies.

If you are walking the shamanic path you need to become your medicine or spirit name. A wonderful way of connecting with your medicine name, and to imbue it with the spirits, is to go and call your name to the directions. Start with a direction that feels good to you.

Hold out your arms and call to the guardians and gatekeepers of that direction and say, 'My name is _____' three times. Then repeat it all to the other three directions. Take your time, for there is no rush. Listen to the elements and feel the nature spirits speaking to you through the trees, birds and animals. Once you have done this cross your hands across your heart and say, 'Great Spirit I wish to become my name. I wish to walk the medicine way.'

# Medicine Wheel – Creating Sacred Space

A medicine wheel represents to the indigenous North American people a sacred space for religious, ritual, healing and teaching purposes. They are the sacred hoops of life playing an important part in one's own life and the life of the tribe or community, as it feeds and nurtures each on a spiritual level. Within a deliberately placed stone circle is a cross of stones, rocks or crystals, which represent the four cardinal directions of East, South, West and North.

When Barbara visited the medicine wheel in the Bighorn National Forest in Wyoming, USA, she was invited into such a circle. She had just finished a Sun Dance ceremony at Wounded Knee, South Dakota, and travelled there to leave her Sun Dance crown and prayer ties. The power that she felt from this sacred place was immense as the spirits called to all who came upon the land.

There are places of power like this one all around the world in different forms and shapes. Older medicine wheels have been dated back to 4,500 years old, but nobody really knows for sure what they were used for. Most archaeologists, however, believe them to be used for ceremonial or ritual purposes.

Every medicine wheel is unique, having its own religious philosophy, which will have motivated the people to connect with the spirits and ancestors of the land to construct a sacred site such as this. In 1989 Barbara went to Sedona, Arizona, for the first time. She was called to climb Cathedral Rock and at the top of the mountain was given a vision of a medicine wheel to build. Once built, she stepped inside the wheel and connected to the land, the ancestors and the spirits of nature. As she sat within the circle she felt the wheel lift off the rock and soar above the earth.

She spent the night on the rock on a vision quest, giving her an experience not to be forgotten. Every year she visits the wheel, and each time a stone has been moved, thus creating different shapes. It is a mandala that changes with the people and with nature, shaping a place of sacred space. We have travelled all over the world learning many different medicine wheel philosophies. The directions, the elements, the crystals, the animals are all different wherever you travel throughout the world.

Back on her homeland, Barbara was called to go to the Bronze Age Nine Ladies stone circle on Stanton Moor, Derbyshire. As she sat within the magical circle, which dates back thousands of years, she asked which medicine wheel teachings she should follow. This is what she was told:

Wherever you go, connect with the spirits and ancestors of the land you are upon. Ask them what they would like you to do, for you will be tapping into the ancestor soul of the very land you stand upon. Then when you feel you are ready, create your own sacred circle with stones, wood, feathers, whatever you feel called to do. Now sit within the circle and face each direction in turn. Note how you feel, and how the directions affect you. Become aware of the elements in each direction too. How do they make you feel? What messages are you receiving? What do you need to learn? This is a magical circle created by your spirit combined with the spirits of nature. This way you become one with all around you.

This felt so familiar to Barbara as she was brought up in the tradition of creating a magical circle. She would walk around in a circle of natural beauty whilst holding her staff. A staff is rather like a long walking stick carved out of specific wood, chosen for its properties suitable to the user. It is used as a tool in ritual and ceremony in one's spiritual journey and symbolises authority, power and leadership. She would visualise the circle to create a sacred space and form a magical protection around her. By casting her own circle she felt protected and safe.

Our ancestors have been creating the magic on the land for thousands of years using the same principles as ourselves. It is the intention that is the most important aspect, the focus, the ability to create a cone of power and to call on the spirits that creates your very own medicine wheel.

In her shamanic faery work, Flavia creates and uses a medicine wheel to create sacred space and to call in and connect with the elemental beings who are associated with each of the four directions. As with most medicine wheels the circle is divided into quarters. She starts at the North, facing that direction and calls upon the gatekeepers of that direction, the element of Earth and the elemental guardians, the gnomes. In this quarter she connects with all that North, Earth and gnomes represent before moving round to the East, then South and finally the West – each one connecting to the relevant element and its guardian elemental and all that they are associated with. It's a wonderful way to connect with the magic of nature and to call upon the advice and guidance of the faery realm, as well as honouring it too. By sitting in certain quarters one can also learn about current feelings as well as any blocks that one may have in relation to that quarter's full meanings (for full details check out her book *Way of the Faery Shaman* by Moon Books).

Creating your own medicine wheel does not have to be difficult. The most important factor is to know where the directions are and then let the spirits of the land guide and teach you. Be sure to allow your natural intuition to guide you, remembering that it is your intention from your heart that is the most sacred of all.

## 22

# Plant Medicine Teachers

There is a lot of controversy about the use of planet medicines in shamanic practice, and yet Shamans have been using hallucinogenic plant teachers for thousands of years. The spirit of the plant has been communicating with Shamans, healers and medicine teachers in this ancient form of shamanic practice. When the spirits of the plant medicine call to you there is no going back.

The plant medicine, such as ayahuasca, which is a psychoactive plant medicine, is used for cleansing and curing illness and disease as part of indigenous shamanic practices. This 'vine of the soul' heals to a very deep level, allowing the facilitation of the spirits of the plant to retrieve and heal the soul of the person receiving the medicine.

Barbara was 40 years old before she experienced her first plant medicine teacher. She was on a trip to Peru and spent a whole week of preparing for receiving the teaching from the vine of the soul. When asked why it had taken her so long to try out these medicine she said, 'I was never called to try anything hallucinogenic because I had listened to many people, including my parents and social media, about the damaging effects of these drugs, as they called them.' However, she was about to discover a whole different world to the demonic stigma that surrounded plant medicine. At the top of Machu Picchu a Shaman handed her an Inti plant medicine. Having smoked it she had a brand new sight. As she looked around Machu Picchu she could see a grid system around and through the Earth, she could see everyone's aura and into their bodies, enabling her to see any illness or disease. For her, attachments could be seen from people to people and from the spirit world and in that moment she just knew. For the next six months she travelled around South and North

American. She met peyote road men, medicine people who would appear out of nowhere saying the plant medicine teachers wished her to work with them. By doing so her mediumship abilities increased tenfold, as well as her healing and divination abilities. She was able to see, feel and know to a far greater depth than ever before.

Flavia experienced something similar when initiated by Barbara herself some years later in the way of plant medicine teachers. Her natural connection with the elemental realm increased dramatically, as did her abilities to hear and see the divinatory messages of nature and the spirit world.

Many people approach us and ask us our views on taking plant medicines. Before embarking on this great teaching it is best to prepare yourself on a mental, emotional and spiritual level before approaching a Shaman with a view to the partaking of these medicines. It is important to travel to the land where the medicine comes from and work with the native teachers who know how to prepare these medicines in the correct way. We must stress that we do not advocate, in any way whatsoever, the taking of plant medicine away from the land, the spirits and the ancestors of where it has been grown. Each plant medicine is connected to the soil, the water, the air, the sun and the spirit of its homeland. To take the medicine away from its natural habitat takes away the very spirit of the medicine itself.

Unfortunately we have known of such happenings and have observed dire consequences all because the medicine was not correctly honoured and respected on a land that was foreign to the medicine itself. If you wish to make a journey to work with these plants, embark on a vision quest to ask for answers such as which medicine, land and teacher would suit you at this time.

These medicines are not to be used for fun, or just to try it out. It is important to honour the process. These teacher plants show us our full potential and were put on this planet for us to discover and work with. They are the food of the gods! They cure many people of pain and depression and give us the ability to explore our own unique psyches. Unfortunately the establishment doesn't want us to discover our full potential, they want to keep us in the dark about the benefits of these great teachers, which is one of the reasons they are so taboo.

Plant medicines need to be used in ceremony, not recreationally. There have been many times when we have had to heal and do soul retrieval work on people who had been misguided and used the medicine incorrectly under poor supervision. The people concerned felt frightened as they were not grounded or centred and some had been totally removed from their physical bodies.

This is where it can get dangerous. There are many out there declaring themselves as Shamans, but with no proper training or understanding of how the plant medicine is used, and why. Of course the choice is yours. But we will advise you to not be forced into anything you don't want to do. Don't take these medicines because it the 'in thing' to do or because you want to look cool. Most importantly avoid mixing your medicines! Don't drink alcohol with them or smoke tobacco with the medicine. Plant medicines are to be used on their own, separately.

There will always be many people on different sides of the fence for and against. If you have not experienced the medicine then don't knock it or say it is wrong. If you have a bad experience with the medicine ask yourself if it was the medicine or perhaps the way it was handled, for example with no honour, respect or prayers before use.

There are many different paths that we all choose to walk upon. None of them are wrong, for within each is a great teaching that leads you to wherever you are going. If you feel drawn to work with plant medicine teachers make sure your feet are firmly planted on the earth. Ask if it will serve your highest purpose and then listen for the answer on the winds. If you find yourself booking a ticket to South America then you know you are on the start of a journey that will lead you to your soul. Have no expectations, do not plan anything, just turn up and allow the ancestors and spirits of the land to guide you.

## 23

# Power Animals and Allies

For many in the shamanic traditions it is believed that the spirits of animals walk with us from the time we are born. They protect and guide us, assisting with journeying and through illness. Their power, coupled with that of the Shaman, is powerful medicine indeed. The Shaman calls on spirit animals to watch over and guide them through the maze of life. From the moment we leave the Summerlands these amazing animal spirits watch over us.

Children are naturally drawn to animals. Where our ancestors would have lived among wild animals, today cats, dogs and other domesticated pets have taken their place to live as part of the family. Any living creature can serve us as an ally, and does serve if we choose to acknowledge them in our lives, from the tiniest ant whose medicine is just as powerful as a wolf or bear. Plants and trees can also serve as plant spirit guides.

Throughout life you will find that your power animals may change or you might call upon a certain animal to help and assist you when needed. You will find they stay with you for the duration of your life, or for the time period in which you need their medicine. Whether the animal is a mammal, four legged, two legged, winged or insect, they are all just as important as each other. Many people often ask us if a dragon, unicorn or other mythical creature can be a power animal, and of course, the answer is 'Yes!' We have also found that some people have prehistoric animals and extinct beings, such as the dodo, as their power animals. Just because the animals are dead in this physical plane does not mean they do not exist in another form, for their energy still lives on in the other-worlds and therefore are very much alive.

Flavia has always had an affinity with rooks, having nursed their injured young when she was a child. Since then rooks have been her power animal, as well as her others who include snake, dog, wolf, elephant, dragon and unicorn. In 2012, however, a new spirit animal visited her in the dreamtime. She had taken her Faery Shaman workshops nationwide and felt an overwhelming desire to colour her beautiful natural blonde hair bright red! That night she slept deeply and in the dreamtime was surprised to find a bright red and orange salamander looking up at her as he lay heavily on her solar plexus chakra, in her midriff. Even though Flavia worked regularly with these elemental guardians of fire, she really did not want him there and asked him to move. He would not budge! She screamed out for Barbara to remove him. She refused, explaining to her, in the dream, that the salamander would only move when his work was done. The next day she was giving a talk at a Faery Fayre. At the end of the session a gentleman approached her and handed her a gift, telling her that he didn't know what the significance was or why he was giving this to her. She opened the little jewelled box that housed the gift and pulled out a silver chain with a pendant of a brightly coloured salamander dangling from it. She had got the message loud and clear and embraced the salamander medicine that offers her the courage, strength and passion she needs to fulfil her life purpose and destiny.

Barbara's first power animal came to her when she was a child growing up in the Highlands of Scotland. She would sit with the ravens in the forest behind the house of her mentor, Swein, and talk with them. Swein gave Barbara the name Raven as her pagan or earth-centred name. She currently walks with snake, bear, owl, elephant, fly and wolf, alongside raven and hawk.

Cat medicine plays a very big part in both our lives too. Anubis is a beautiful sleek black cat who we rescued as a kitten at Yule in 2013. He shares our home in Derbyshire and we are sure he is really a black panther in disguise!

Which type of animal plays a big part in your life? Do you find that animals are naturally drawn to you? If so, which ones in particular? Not so long ago animals and humans were closely linked. Then gradually the connection was lost due to the fragmentation of tribes and clans as people became incorporated into towns and city life.

You will find that when needed the spirits of the animals will come to you to offer their assistance. For example, if you need strength and courage the bear spirit could appear to you. If you need a clear picture of a situation and cannot get clarity then call on the spirit of eagle or hawk to assist you. They will come in the dreamtime to give you visions, they will cross your path and may even come into your home. If an animal seems to randomly turn up then you will need to interpret the message it brings with its medicine or energy.

Most people do not realise that when a bird comes tapping on your window it is a message from Spirit. Messages from animals can come in any form. You may switch on the TV to find a wildlife programme being aired, or keep seeing pictures of a particular animal everywhere you go and sometimes you may find yourself chasing out any that have come into your home uninvited, such as ants, insects and mice. All animals bring with them a message from Spirit. Those who recognise this under-stand why they have come.

It's important to communicate like Doctor Doolittle and 'talk to the animals'. Barbara was visiting her friend, Alison, in New York and as they were chatting on the sofa, Alison let out a loud scream. 'It's that mouse again! He's sitting over there,' she cried.

Barbara looked across to the mouse and simply said, 'Time to go little one,' and turned back to carry on talking. Minutes later her friend screamed that the mouse was sitting at her front door. Barbara opened the door and the mouse scurried outside. Alison hated the job she was in, but was too scared of change even though she had the opportunity. 'Mouse' came into her life to teach her not to overlook the obvious and over analyze. But being over emotional she found the most mundane and simplest of tasks extremely difficulty. Mouse left because she had not seen the message being given and so Barbara set him free from his obligation. Barbara's friend never did see mouse ever again, she regretted not taking the opportunity to change job and now looks everywhere she goes for her animal allies, promising never to ignore them again. Have you had an animal come calling that you have ignored? Time to rectify this situation...

**Power Animal Journey**
Take your drum if you have one or play a shamanic drumming CD (details can be found in the back of this book). Find a quiet place where you will not be disturbed and make yourself comfortable. Ensure the room is dark or cover your eyes with a blindfold or scarf. Start the CD or begin drumming. Become aware of the sound of the drum as it carries you downwards into the earth. Imagine a large cave with an entrance. You make your way down into this entrance using candle light to illuminate your way. Deeper and deeper down you go until you come across a large opening into a huge underground cave.

Here you feel the presence of another being, but you do not feel afraid. Through the darkness you see a pair of eyes shining back at you. You ask quietly and gently if this being is your power animal. They will only show themselves to you if they are. You might find that more than one appears. At this point don't be disappointed if your expectations are not met. Many people have ideas and thoughts of what they would like as a power animal. Once they reveal themselves, let them come forward slowly. It's important you trust this process as you might feel as if you are making this up. Please know that you are not. Remember to not dismiss any animal that comes to you, for they are coming to you to help assist you in your current situation.

Get a sense and feeling of why they are here and again ask if they are your power animal. If they continue to come forward, look into their eyes and feel the strength and qualities coming from them. Spend time in this underground cave with them, get to know them. Become your animal, feel how they use their sensing abilities – their smell, their sight, their hearing, their absolute knowing.

When it feels right, thank your power animal for revealing themselves to you. They may retreat back into the cave or start the journey back with you to the Middle World. Take your time.

Once back in the room that you started in, sit with the knowledge that you have made your first contact with your power animal.

Having established who your power animal is you may find that you are drawn to buy, or may acquire or are gifted, amulets, necklaces, parts of your animal, pictures, statues or objects. You may discover now as you look around your home that your power animal has been with you all along in many various forms.

Barbara has raven wings gifted to her, hawk wings, a wolf skin and a bear tooth necklace gifted at Sun Dance. While on our travels we jump at the chance to have boa constrictors, pythons and any other types of snakes we can find wrapped around our necks, much to the horror of onlookers. But we know and love snakes, as we do any animal, and understand the medicine they offer. As a shamanic practitioner you can use any pictures, skins or feathers you may have to help in both the healing of yourself or the healing of others.

During a trip to the Far East we were honoured to be gifted the sacred skin of a king cobra, having witnessed the shedding of it before our very eyes. That skin is now used by us, when performing shamanic healing, for when snake medicine needs to be called upon.

The art of becoming your animal is to call on them to help you through life's journeys. Below is a list of the most common power animals. Again it is determined by which continent you live on. If, for example, you live in the UK and your power animal is a kangaroo, look deeply into why it is with you and for what purpose. Perhaps you need to visit Australia or it could be that you need its medicine for a particular reason. It is you that needs to ask the questions and to listen deeply for the answers. There are many hundreds of animal allies, and these power animals vary from Shaman to Shaman. Below is a short list covering the most popular animals, including those who are extinct and mythical. It covers their qualities, abilities and what they can mean for you.

**Bear:** Fearless medicine. Stand up for what you believe in, no matter what challenges you face be steadfast and sure. Balance between all seasons, light and dark. Look for solitude and quietness in winter. Seek new opportunities in the spring and summer. It allows time for introspection in the autumn to birth dreams and visions.

**Butterfly:** Invites change and transformation. It brings the ability to change in any given situation. It promotes being consciously connected to Spirit at all times, through feeling, seeing, sensing and knowing. Receive joy into your life. Trust that change is a good thing. It enables you to see the bigger picture, paving the way for soul evolution and growth.

**Cat:** Encourages curiosity, discovery of unknown places, people and circumstances. Cat is independent, completely self-assured and clever. Unpredictable and mysterious, it offers many lives within lives.

**Deer:** Promotes gentleness and love. It brings support and care, in teaching how to love both yourself and others.

Compassionate for others. Deer helps develop keen sensitivity for peace, love, happiness and joy. Be swift and alert. It helps us see the cause of shadows.

**Dinosaur:** Invokes ancient wisdom, is fearless and offers clear vision in the pursuit of goals. Dinosaur is able to digest all aspects of an issue, offering strength and tenacity.

**Dodo:** Hides behind naivety and is a reminder not to trust everything you hear. Can fuel aggression and be judgmental.

**Dog:** Faithful and loyal, promoting friendship and companionship. Dog serves without wanting anything in return. It is devoted to its nearest and dearest and offers playfulness and joy.

**Dolphin:** Offers knowledge as the decoder of ancient symbols and information of the cosmos. It brings play, fun and laughter and a reminder that life is not always a serious undertaking; encourages all to spend time at the ocean. Cleanse and heal with the power of water.

**Dragon:** The diffuser of anger. Dragon invokes passion for achieving life purpose. It offers strength, personal power and confidence, and acts as the revealer of truth, ancient wisdoms and mystical arts.

**Eagle:** Brings the ability to see the greater vision with speed and fortitude. It reaffirms connection to spirit teachers and guides. It is a sacred messenger of healing by seeing into spiritual truths. Power and balance in all things.

**Horse:** Ensures victory through confidence. It offers elegance and stature, a carrier through troublesome times. Horse also represents companions and friends, for help is at hand. Spirit messenger between the worlds; freedom to ride on the winds.

**Lion:** Offers strength, personal power and assertiveness. Lion helps with the struggle of dealing with one's inner feelings, assists in controlling anger and rage, both towards others and if directed at oneself. Premonition warns of a threatening event or situation.

**Mouse:** Helps to bring about accomplishment without attention and fuss. Egoless, reserved and shy. It assists those who make the simplest task fraught with difficulty. Fearful of life. Need to focus on the big things in life to remove trivia. Mouse navigates danger.

**Owl:** Offers wisdom to see all sides from different perspectives. It is a gatekeeper to the Akashic records. Owl is a keen observer and keeps silent through all difficulties. Great intuition and keeper of secrets, facilitates great discretion.

**Panther:** Protective and nurturing. Panther assists in reclaiming one's personal power. It is a walker during the dark night of the soul and offers a deep and profound understanding of death. The ability to make quick decisive actions. It suggests the need to pace oneself to stand the course.

**Raven:** The keeper of secrets, master magician and shape shifter. Raven awakens inner mysticism and interprets animal language. It provides a shift in consciousness in all situations. Continual change and spiritual awakening comes easily through raven.

**Snake:** The symbol of death and rebirth, shedding the illusion of fear. It removes limitations in order to see one's true potential. Makes sense of matters of sexuality and fertility. Creator of the great mysteries of life, assists healing and promotes wisdom. Symbolises eternity. Remover of obstacles and fears.

**Spider:** Weaves the web of fate and fortune. Brings balance between past and future destiny. Spider awakens creativity and assists in the ability to weave one's web without interference from others. The power to create destiny. Entanglement removed from people and situations.

**Swan:** Enables psychic abilities. Brings inner grace, poise and balance. To know and acknowledge one's own inner beauty. Awakens the power of self-knowing. Swan is fiercely courageous and protects its young. It represents understanding of one's inner innocence. Assists in developing intuitive abilities.

**Unicorn:** Opens the heart and brings pure, divine love. Unicorn is a carrier to the elemental kingdom and connection with nature spirits. It indicates a life purpose in assisting gifted children and assists in opening up intuitive abilities. Helps develop the heart chakra. It represents peace, love and creativity.

**Wolf:** Injects the spirit of wilderness, understands true self-sufficiency and the ability to adapt to change. Deep loyalty and honouring of family values come with wolf. It assists in bringing balance between being too dependent or independent. Harmony and discipline in all things, helps to avoid trouble and confrontations. It has the ability to pass on wisdom and to teach others.

If your animal is not in this list, take the time to find out what it represents. Of course, you can Google your animal or buy a book on power animals, but try to tune in and find out what your animal represents to you and for you. One thing to remember is that no two animals are alike. No two dogs are alike, no two bears are alike, no two ants are alike. They all have unique individual characters, just as we humans do. The best way is to meet your power animal in person. You can either travel to their native lands, as we do, to spend time with your power animal and get to know them, or go to a zoo where you can find most of the animals from around the world.

We love the heart energy of elephants and experienced this medicine when we stayed with a herd in Indonesia. We found that they exuded patience and unconditional selflessness. The peace we received in our hearts from just being in their presence was sublime. One elephant, Ellie, was extremely ill, and so was Flavia when we arrived to spend time with them. When the two of them met, Ellie stretched out her trunk and grabbed Flavia's arm. With a firm grip Ellie then pulled hard and released the trunk, in exactly the same way as a Shaman would perform extraction. The sickness was pulled from Flavia's body and she instantly felt better. That night we both kept vigil for Ellie until dawn, when we discovered that she was up on her feet and feeding. She joined the rest of the herd later that day.

Animal medicine is all around us and is offered freely with no judgment or conditions. The next time you watch birds fly across the sky look to what they are and feel their medicine. When a dog bounds up to lick you, accept his gift of loyalty, affection and companionship. And instead of swatting a fly when it lands on you, try to decipher why he has come to you and what message he is trying to convey.

**24**

# Protection

Whenever we do any shamanic work it is vital we protect ourselves. It is good practice to call in protection every day, whether consciously working with the spirit world, or not. Before partaking in any work with Spirit, be it meditation or invocation, you must 'ground' yourself, so that you are anchored within your body and are kept connected to this Earth realm. Going into nature and standing barefooted on the ground will instantly ground and connect you. Or, wherever you are, imagine strong roots growing down from the soles of your feet burying deep into the ground, your roots growing stronger and longer until they reach the centre of the Earth. Visualise a huge crystal, take notice of what it looks like, and allow your roots to wrap around it. Breathe up the crystalline energy, breathe up the Earth magic and allow it surge through every cell, every vessel, every part of your very being. You are now grounded, and ready to connect.

Drawing a circle, whether physically or in the mind's eye, is a strong form of protection. It can guard you against unwanted energies from other people, such as psychic attacks, negative thought forms and from locations, such as old buildings. In order to connect with the world of Spirit the Shaman understands how important it is to be a clear channel, which means being free of negativity and fear. Simply imagining a circle surrounding you will immediately give you the protection that is required. Other ways include visualising a circle in front of you, or drawing in the air with your power finger (the index finger of whichever is your dominant hand). See it growing to a little bigger than the size of you and then step into it. Or you may wish to use the following visualisation, which will ground, centre and protect you before taking up any magical work:

## Protection, Grounding and Centring Ceremony

Stand with your feet slightly apart and firmly on the ground. See, in your mind's eye, your roots (as explained above) growing deeply into the Earth below you and allow them to anchor. Feel the strong and grounding Earth energy as you connect with the element of Earth.

You become aware of a soft breeze caressing your body as the Guardians of Air surround you. Breathe in the air deeply. Feel and welcome this precious lifegiver as it enters your lungs. You become aware of a light, refreshing rain landing upon you. Embrace the Guardians of Water, who have come to cleanse and purify you. A fluffy white cloud moves in the sky, to reveal the Sun in all its glory. The Guardians of Fire beat down their burning rays upon you. Feel the delicious warmth, nurturing and healing your body.

With the power of all four elements connecting with every part of you, feel yourself merge with each one of them. Now draw on the strength of this energy, feel the power surge though every part of you as you raise your arms. Stand like a star and feel your spirit soar. You are the Earth, the Air, the Fire, the Water and Spirit. Now see yourself circled with a protective energy. You are now grounded, centred and fully protected.

## 25

# Rebirthing

In December 2004 Barbara became seriously ill and was rushed into hospital. After three days she was still experiencing a high fever and so the doctors gave her antibiotics, but to no avail. During the night of Yule, 21st December, she fell into a deep coma and was given a 50/50 chance of survival. Her friends kept vigil around her bedside all that night until sunrise, when finally her fever subsided and she shared with them what she had experienced. Here is her story:

> I fell into a deep, dark tunnel dropping down and down until I reached the bottom. I struggled and fought as beings, very much like gargoyles, started to rip me apart. My skin came off, then my muscles, all the way down to the bone. It was a very strange feeling, not painful, but very uncomfortable. I was just my skeleton. Then in front of me came my life review showing me all that I have done in this lifetime including the people I had hurt and the lies I told as a child, nothing was missed out. I was then shown all my past lives and again all the things I had done that were not deemed as good. In that moment I 'got it'. As soon as the realisation hit me I started to spin. I felt myself being lifted upwards as my body was given new muscles and skin. The next thing I knew was I was fully back in my body, in the hospital bed.

This was a death of the old and a rebirthing of the new. From then on Barbara felt totally different. All her feelings of guilt, fear and shame had been stripped away and she was reborn. Many people will experience this form of rebirthing. Those who are called onto the shamanic path sometimes find that a serious illness bestows them with that experience. You will find that a life-threatening event will change your life forever, but will gift you with newfound abilities and strengths, thus removing the fears and pains that have held you back for far too long.

For many people a sickness, of both the mind and the body, will continue until they answer the 'call' of the ancestors. When they do they become aware of Spirit, become more sensitive, enabling them to follow their destiny. Sadly today many people go through this rite of passage with no comprehension of the teachings, or to be open to any learning.

This process of rebirth allows one to journey both into the inner and outer worlds. This in itself is a great teacher to help you learn about your body, your biology, your mental aptitude and spiritual tenacity. It also gives you a new understanding of others' suffering, enabling you to see into their body and root out the causes of their original wounding. Rebirthing can of course come in any forms. Spirit does not always require one to suffer physical pain. But it will always require some form of 'death' to the old.

Having comfortably run a healing practice for many years, in her home town that she had never left, Spirit called to Flavia to leave behind all that she had built up in her business, and all that she loved, including her dear husband, her home, possessions, family and friends to completely start again, from scratch. This required absolute trust and great strength of character to be able to step away from her comfort zone and into the unknown. It took more than two years to completely shed the grief, guilt and sorrow that she had endured from leaving behind all that she knew, in order to step fully into the destiny that the ancestors had in store for her. It was as though she was blind for that time, not knowing where and what she was being led to, but all the while she completely trusted in the Great Mystery. Only when she was truly freed, in every sense, from any fears was she led out of the dark forest and into the light where a new shining and glorious path of the Shaman awaited.

Pain is a great teacher, in whatever form, and instead of running away from it we must face it and push through to the other side of the pain itself. When we do this, the effect causes us to go into a semi-induced state of being, connecting us with the ancestor spirits who direct us through the process of initiation into becoming a Shaman. What both of us experienced was 'dismemberment' and then 'rememberment'.

Many will have gone through rebirthing without under-standing or realising the effects of this form of deep healing, which Shamans and those going through their apprenticeship have experienced over thousands of years. Many similar stories from all over the world, from Siberia to Africa and Peru to Greenland, tell of individuals who have experienced similar initi-ations through their calling to become a Shaman. These Shamans may not have a lineage or live in traditional societies, however, when the spirits call you they must be answered, for it is in the very essence of your being to do so.

Usually a devastating situation causes the 'victim' to surface. You may feel sorry for yourself, expect others to put you first or become angry with the world. This is not the way of the Shaman.

Time to step out of being this mentality and look at why you may be suffering a recurring injury, illness, depression or situation. Write a list of what you are experiencing and going through it and your mental reactions. For instance, are you blaming someone or something for your situation? Is it causing you to feel miserable, angry or even betrayed? Time to look deeper. What lessons could be learned from this? Could you summon the strength to let go and trust in order to move forward. Spirit teaches in many ways. It is time to discover what they are telling you, for freedom beckons. If you feel that you would like to let go of anything that no longer serves you then light a candle. As you gaze into the flame say:

I call upon the Spirits of Fire, bring me your courage and all I desire. Ignite the flame of passion within, so I can connect with the strength of the djinn.

With honour, respect, I call upon you. Please help me to work my life purpose through. Extinguish the dark that blacks out the light, so I am released of fears and my plight. Allow the fire to ravage through me, to purify, cleanse and set me free. I am of power, this I now know, as I become the sacred glow.

Dear beings of light, of summer and Sun, with my heart I give thanks.

There, it is done.

Feel yourself getting warmer as you watch the flame expand and become embraced within the vivid colours of red, gold and orange. Connect with the power and the life-giving force of fire while every breath fills your entire body, awakening every cell. Now tell the flame all that you wish to have assistance with, of any fears and worries. As the flame licks away old hurts and wounds they are replaced by a sacred glow. Now take a deep breath in as the glow ignites the fire energy within you. It rages through every part of your body, purging you of all negative influences. As the fire grows it consumes the very essence of all problems and fears, replacing them with passion and desire enabling you to stand strong, to fearlessly step towards your dreams and goals. When you feel that this is completed blow out the candle and let the swirl of the extinguished flame wrap around you.

## 26

# Rites of Passage

A rite of passage is a ceremony or ritual that marks the transition from one phase of life to another, often helped by an individual, elder or group of people. In the present day this form of assistance is not readily available for the majority of people due to the lack of skills and resources. We have all experienced rites of passage throughout our lives, without even necessarily realising it.

Life transitions take many forms and start immediately with our birth into this world, which for some can be very traumatic. The next major stage in life is puberty, which again can be very frightening for both girls and boys if they do not have a responsible adult or elder around to explain what is happening. The trauma of going from primary school to secondary school can be very scary too, especially if you are leaving your friends behind. Graduating and going out into the big world to work, for a lot of young adults who have not been schooled in street wisdom, is indeed a hard playground to be initiated into.

Meeting a love partner, finding your soulmate in whatever form they may come, be it boy-girl, boy-boy, girl-girl, is in itself an intense rite of passage and one that not many young adults are prepared for. Marriage is a major rite of passage, especially for those who don't have a choice about to whom they are betrothed. Arranged marriages can be very harrowing and stressful if the person is not honed into these ways and traditions. Nevertheless, marriage for even the most loved-up couples is still a transition from singledom to being very much part of a couple. It marks the leaving of one's parents to step into responsibility and adulthood.

For women, childbirth is a huge transition from maiden to motherhood. Usually for both parents it is a time of great joy, but with this too comes stress. Most parents are young adults and are not prepared for the responsibilities, hard work and changes to lifestyle that come with a new child.

The very last rites of passage, that none of us can escape from, is the death of the body. Of course, when we are young we are in complete denial and the thought of death doesn't occur to us. For the elderly, death is what they often focus on, and tend to shut themselves away to wait for the inevitable to happen.

Each rite of passage should be celebrated or acknowledged as notable milestones, not something to be ashamed of, or ignored. Sadly today no-one is encouraged to fully embody or incorporate these rites of passage into their lives.

Youngsters are not encouraged to take responsibility for decisions that will set their life path for their future. They need a sense of their own story through self-exploration. This is necessary in providing space to transit and embrace core values and role responsibilities appropriate to the initiate's stage of life.

As decades and centuries have rolled by the new generations tend to mark and recognise their rites of passage by their first drink binge, first sexual encounter, extreme sports and pushing the boundaries of respectability with people in authority and those who have gone before them.

## 27

# Shapeshifters

As a child Barbara heard stories of selkies. They would live as seals in the sea until they wanted to come onto the land, when they would shed their skins and become like humans. This great legend sparked her imagination. Every time she went onto the land she would see birds and animals and imagine what it was like to fly like the raven, run like a deer, to feel what they felt. It was an incredible feeling to experience becoming one with the animals.

Today everywhere we look in books and films, we see shapeshifting being played out in fantasy fiction. It is as if we have come full circle, for in mythology and folklore, since recorded history, shapeshifters have played a big part in our lives. From the *Epic of Gilgamesh* and the *Iliad* to Norse sagas and Irish Celtic legends, shapeshifting is described as the ability to change from a deity or human form into an animal or vice versa. By going under this guise, Shamans travelled long distances to spy on foreign lands for their ruler. This is a form of totemism, stemming back thousands of years to when the connection between animals and the Shaman was an intimate relationship. The bond of friendship and protection between them was intense, a close connection of life and death. Finally, when one died, the same fate would befall the other.

This is metamorphosis in its highest form. Greek mythology has many stories of shapeshifting; however, they saw it as a punishment from the gods who changed them. Athena transformed Arachne into a spider, Zeus changed Lycaon into a wolf, Artemis caused Actaeon to become a stag and so it goes on. In the book series *The Chronicles of Narnia*, humans are changed into animals until they learn the error of their ways and only then are they transformed back.

Shapeshifting has a common theme throughout the world, played out in poems, verses and storytelling. Stories abound of witches in the Middle Ages transforming into cats or hares, as their familiars. Fairies and wizards were also noted for their shapeshifting abilities. Barbara remembers sitting round a fire in Taos, New Mexico. A Navajo peyote road man told stories of the Navajo skin walkers who have the powers to travel in animal form. It was a beautiful night listening to the stories, the stars were shining brightly and the moon was full. Suddenly everything changed. The wind whipped up around them and they could feel a presence. It was eerie and the hairs pricked up on the back of Barbara's neck. She said to the peyote road man, Alberto Snr, that she felt a strange energy behind her, rather like a wolf. The next minute a wolf howled. Alberto said, 'That will be the skin walkers keeping an eye on us.'

They all felt the real tangible power as it floated through the air, charging it with electrifying energy and as though the skin walker was reading their thoughts. The next minute a comet came from the sky. It was like headlights on full beam shining upon them. As it passed the wind died down and stillness once more came upon the land. Barbara has travelled all over the world and has seen many things, but that night on the land of Taos, New Mexico, she came to know, sense and feel the true art of shapeshifting in all its power and strength. It is not a myth; it is very real and very much alive.

Today Shamans and shamanic practitioners use shapeshifting abilities to change their perception e.g.; to have the eyes of a hawk in order to see into the body, to root out sickness and disease. By working with your power animal you can take on their abilities and senses. Flavia was driving along a country single-track lane when a large van came hurtling towards her. There was no place in the road to pull in, nor was there time to. Instinctually she drew herself in as she quickly took upon mouse medicine to make herself smaller, and even squeaked! Miraculously she wasn't hit and the van passed her without a scratch.

When we both visited the Grand Canyon we watched the huge black ravens flying over the mountain tops and swooping down across the great ravine. Can you imagine being able to see what these birds can see? Well, that's just what we did! As we took a deep breath we became one with the ravens. It was exhilarating as we flew higher and higher, giving us a breathtaking bird's eye view of the national park itself. *'Fly like a raven, fly so high. Circling the universe, on wings of pure love.'*

Shapeshifting is a wonderful shamanic tool that can help you in your everyday life. If you are sitting in a traffic jam, for instance, then become a bird and fly out across the traffic to see what the hold-up is. You could become a mole to sense what is in the ground beneath you before digging or planting, or shapeshift into a fish as you check out the safety of a pool or lake if you wish to swim in it.

If you would like to shapeshift then choose an animal that you feel you would like to be, your favourite animal or one that would suit your needs at this moment in time. For instance, if you need strength then choose a lion, a dove for peace or a wolf for protection. You may wish to read up on your chosen animal and have a few artefacts, such as statues or toys of the animal in question, near to you.

Now, with your eyes closed take a deep breath and focus on the characteristics of that animal. Breathe them into your very being and start to feel them. In your mind's eye see the natural surroundings of that animal and imagine that you are there, as the animal itself. As you continue to do this you will be taken on a visual journey, in your mind, as you become one with the animal. Eventually, with practise, you will be able to just take on the feeling of becoming an animal at will. You may find it frightening at first, for you will feel only the body and characteristics of the animal you have become. But do not fear, for the easy transformation back into your own mind and body is assured.

## 28

# Spirit Guardians and Guides

One of the most important attributes of the Shaman, or shamanic practitioner, is their personal spirit guardians or spirit guides. When we journey from the Summerlands to the Earth plane we are connected with our spirit guardians who watch over us on our voyage of discovery called life. A Shaman will contact the spirits by going into an altered state of awareness, a trance, in order to request help in their work for healing purposes and spiritual counselling.

When Barbara was nearly four years old, she awoke to find her first spirit guide at the foot of her bed, watching her. Years later she was to find out that he was a Native American guide called Touch the Clouds. When she visited Arizona years later she walked into a trading post and on the stand was a picture of Touch the Clouds. Barbara has many spirit guides and guardians from around the world from many different cultures.

Flavia, too, experienced something similar during a trip to Arizona, with Barbara years later. Throughout her time there she was receiving visitations from the spirit of a Native American elder, a chief, who she had not encountered before. One day Barbara took her into the very trading post she had stepped into years before, albeit unknown to Flavia. As she walked around the store she came face to face with a picture of the very same chief she had been visited by. She called to Barbara and explained that she had been visited by this man, in spirit form, many times since they had stepped foot onto the native lands. Barbara told her it was Red Cloud, a chief of the Oglala Lakota. He was a very strong war leader who fought for his land and people from 1868 to 1909. Flavia felt very honoured indeed, and he continues to be her guide in her shamanic work and way of life.

What we find very interesting is that a lot of people who call themselves Shamans, or shamanic practitioners, do not seem to know who their spirit guides are. They will often admit to not having a connection with Spirit, or not knowing how to connect. Some also believe that it is not important to have a spirit guide. It is very important when you want to work in this field that you first and foremost establish a connection with your guardian and spirit guides, or power animals or allies, before commencing this work.

Without one, it would be like going into a maze of tunnels with no guide to show you where to go and how to get out. You would be trapped and searching for a long time. A spirit guide is your helper on this plane of existence, who wishes for you to be free.

Many people start on this path without having the basic teachings and understanding in place. The first step is attuning to the seven directions of North, East, South, West, Above, Below and Centre, and the guardians and gatekeepers who watch over the gateways.

Each gateway has a presiding spirit or guardian. By standing in each direction you will feel, sense and start to become aware of the different energies associated with the individual directions. Before you start you must ensure your clarity, intention and focus are heightened within yourself before embarking on ceremony or ritual.

The next step in working with the spirits is to take time to get to know and understand the spirits of the elements, and how they play a very important part in our everyday lives. Now you will want to meet your own personal guardian or spirit guide. You may have consciously connected with them since birth, or have an ancestor who is now in the spirit world working as your spirit guide. A spirit guide could also be someone you knew in a previous lifetime or you may have worked with a being in the spirit world who has agreed to watch over you on your return to the Earth plane.

No Shaman ever walks alone, for each step is guided by these wise advisors. It is our choice whether we listen or not. Spirit guides come in many forms including spiritual leaders and mythical heroes and will bring to you many gifts including teachings and protection.

Before coming to this Earth plane we decide, along with spirit, who will be best suited as a guide. We, as humans, cannot choose who we wish to have as permanent animal allies and spirit guides once we get here. So when we need to seek help, in any given situation, we call upon those in the spirit world to help and guide us through the difficult times. If we do call upon a specific guide to help us, then they will choose and accept the responsibility of looking after us if suitable and as and when we need them. We cannot demand or command that they look after us and when.

A wonderful way to connect with your guardians and spirit guides is to sit with a drum, state your intention to the spirit world and start drumming. Decide who you would wish to call upon to help and assist you and for what purpose. It's important to take your time to make your connection, and to trust what you see and feel. The reason we use the drum is to stop the internal thinking process, the monkey chatter mind, so you can use your shamanic abilities and journey to the world of the spirits and ancestors.

Your spirit guide or guardian will only have your best interests at heart. They will be caring, strong, loving. They will never force you to do anything that is beyond your capabilities for they know how far you can stretch yourself. Your guides know your soul, your spirit, the very essence of who you have been and will become in this lifetime. The most important aspect of working with spirit is to trust and believe that they are working with you for your highest good. Without this the relationship will flounder on rocky shores. This should be a two-way communication, with both benefiting from each other. It is relationship of giving and receiving for both. Give thanks of your appreciation for your guides, for watching over you and for creating a wonderful spirit link for you both.

### Connecting with your Spirit Guide

If you are unsure of how to connect with your spirit guide, find a place at home, or in nature, where you won't be disturbed. Now take a deep breath and close your eyes. Bring your focus to your heart and continue to breathe deeply in and out until you feel relaxed. Using your intention to connect with your spirit guide, begin to feel its presence around and within you. You will start to feel the energy of beauty and of love in your heart centre. This is the place of connection. Now bring your imagination into play, for this is where pictures from spirit are placed. Who or what do you see? Is it an animal or a person? If it's a person, what do they look like? Check out their clothing. What era or part of the world are they from? Now breathe in their very essence. Feel it in your heart. Then breathe love from your heart to your guide. Again, breathe in their essence, and breathe back your love. This will start to build up your relationship on a strong energy level, as well as your love for them. Their love for you is unquestionable. Once you feel ready, start to ask them questions. Listen for an immediate response. The first answer is always correct, as after this your ego may kick in and scream, 'You're making this all up!' Please know that your ego is a deceiver and that all that you see and feel is very real indeed, it's just on another level that you aren't familiar with – yet! Once you have finished any communion with your guide, always show your appreciation by saying thank you.

# The Shaman

The Shaman is someone who, along the path of life, has experienced first-hand teachings, rites of passage and some form of death and rebirth, which have changed their life forever. It is not an easy life and not one to be taken lightly. For with the title 'Shaman' comes a heavy responsibility, not only to ourselves, but also to our family, friends and community in which we live.

Today in our ever-changing world there has been a resurgence of shamanism, which is one of the oldest authentic spiritual practices in the world. There are emerging practitioners who are calling themselves Shamans without undergoing any rites of passage, teachings or initiations and when asked about their lineage, or who taught them, cannot respond other than to keep saying that they are Shamans! The name Shaman seems to be the 'in thing' at the moment to call oneself – and not much different from an untrained person to declare themselves as a master teacher, guru or magi.

For the general public, who are looking for a bona fide healer, this can be very risky. It is like going to a doctor seeking medical advice, placing one's life in their hands without knowing that the so-called doctor has only read one book on the subject, or watched surgery being performed on TV. Would you trust this person to heal your life? Probably not and yet we see similar scenarios played out, over and over again. It takes years to walk this path, it is a great responsibility that is not to be taken lightly, because it is life-changing, death defying and mind altering. To walk the path of the Shaman is to be present in the moment 24 hours a day, seven days a week. To be fully aware of these amazing ancient cultural values takes great courage and respect. Shamanism is the most challenging, but rewarding, path you can choose.

The word 'Shaman' is said to most likely originate from the Tungusic Evenki language of North Asia. It means one who knows, one who is consumed by the fires of inspiration. There are many interpretations of the word Shaman and of the word Shamanism. This living ongoing tradition has been passed down through the centuries in many forms. The term Shamanism was first heard and used by Western anthropologists after making contact with the ancient religion of the Turks and the Mongolians. This led the anthropologists on a journey to discover that there are many other similar traditions all over the world from Australia, Africa, Far East, South American and most of Europe focused on the healing and treatment of the soul. Their beliefs were focused on rebalancing not just the person's soul, but also the soul collective of the group, tribe or clan.

Today we live in a world of cross-culture experiences. We can travel to work first hand with the different cultures, honouring each one as individual and sacred. Each culture or tradition shares commonalities in this practice, but they also have varying degrees of differences as well. In the Highlands of Scotland these individuals are known as cunning men and woman, or in the Scottish Gaelic, 'fiosaiche', meaning one who knows. In North American they are known as medicine men and women.

There have been many heated debates about using the name 'Shaman'. Some say it is wrong to declare oneself of that name. But who can say with true authenticity and integrity what is actually right or wrong in whatever one decides to call oneself? This is an individual and personal choice, which carries a great personal responsibility, for words have power and names have meanings. Shamanism first and foremost is about the 'knowing of oneself' before attempting to heal others. How can you help others if you do not know yourself inside out, back to front, upside down? The Shaman has many roles and can be seen through all the different cultures and traditions that weave this ancient medicine with modern tools and techniques.

When we look around the Mind, Body, Spirit events that we take part in throughout the year, we see different forms of Shamanism, all segregated and split apart in the different methodologies, and yet they are all under the same roof.

These events are packed with mediums who act as intermediaries between the natural and supernatural worlds, healers in all their different forms curing the sick, and workshops held that incorporate different teachings from around the world. The role of the Shaman is to gain knowledge and wisdom as a seer, a spirit doctor, a psychologist, negotiator, and ceremonialist. 'Mind, Body, Spirit' sums up the purpose of practice of Shamanism – to bring about healing, harmony, balance and wholeness to an individual or group.

Whether you call yourself a Shaman, healer, witch, medicine man, priest, elder, magician or Druid, you are walking the path of an ancient tradition that was not split apart into separate teachings, but originally incorporated all the modalities as one philosophy and one way of life.

Many Shamans come into this lifetime forgetting their life purpose, due to particular circumstances such as blockages from others, that are put in place during their childhood. This is why so many people today are being called by Spirit to walk the shamanic path and it is our responsibility to help and assist these people to restore their soul and spirit to its rightful states. In doing so it restores the balance within oneself and the healer, enabling them to go out with the correct training to help heal others.

Today around the world Shamanism is undergoing a revival and those being called to this way of life need to understand the deep level of these ancient cultural values and belief systems. In our modern world many people are disconnected from their soul, their spirit, with no vision or spiritual conception as to who they are, why they are here and what life is all about.

Adaptability to live shamanically in our everyday lives is the way of the Shaman. By looking within you will discover, beneath the surface, a living tradition that flows through your blood and bones. Your ancestral memory awakens and remembers, and through time you will become 'one who knows'.

## 30

# Trance States

For the Shaman there are many ways to enter altered states of consciousness. These include journeying with the drum, dancing, fasting, prayer, breath control, sleep deprivation and plant medicine teachers. There are also varying levels of trance. This state of flow, or shamanic trance, enables the Shaman to journey into other nonphysical realities to communicate with the spirits and gain valuable information for soul retrievals and healing. It also allows the Shaman to make subtle changes in the Lower or Upper Worlds, which in turn brings about the effect of that change in the Middle World.

To experience trance states you need to let go of the self, the ego, and become one with All That Is. The one thing that holds people back from this experience is the fear of letting go, of not being in control of any given situation. It is very much like sitting in the back seat of a car and letting a complete stranger drive you to an unknown destination. When in trance it is as though everything is completely different. There is a distorted sense of time, no perception, no thinking. You no longer have a body, you are at ease, as the state of flow and you become one with everyone and everything without attachments.

Barbara's first experience of trance was of sitting in a circle with a group of people, developing her mediumship. This is her account of it:

I was aware of going up a tunnel into the sky and arriving in what felt like an old Roman amphitheatre. There were many beings dressed in white who spoke to me in one collective voice. They explained that I had travelled to another dimension, that they were members of the High Grand Council and were here to help me in my work on the Earth plane. The next minute I was rushing down a white tunnel and became aware of my body once more. As soon as I returned to my physical body I started to shake, I was frozen cold. I had blankets placed around me and still I was shaking. It was the most powerful feeling I had ever experienced and took me a long time to ground myself back in the world once again.

Barbara continued to experience more of these trance states and started to work with the drum to journey to deeper levels of trance. At the age of 40 she travelled to South and North America for six months and whilst there experienced trance states through the use of plant medicine teachers. For her it was a life-changing experience. She prepared fully before she entering a plant-induced trance state. When asked why she had waited so long in life before she took the plant medicines she replied:

I was informed by the spirits that I could not partake in the medicines until I was upon the lands where the medicines grew. I was 40 years old and had listened to many people advising me against taking drugs. What I was to discover was that in the correct environment, with Shamans who work with the ancestors and spirits of the land, that the plant spirit medicine was a great teacher. There are no words to describe what I saw and felt. I worked with ayahuasca, San Pedro, peyote and magic mushrooms and the experiences changed my life and my work as a Shaman.

Barbara's next experience of trance was at Sun Dance in South Dakota. There she had many visions due to fasting for four days at a time. Having no food or water for that amount of time and dancing in the sun produces an incredible trance state.

As a trained classical dancer, Flavia is no stranger to the movement and energy of dance. However, it wasn't until she first danced to the beat and sounds of the shamanic drums that she truly took to the floor, literally! As the drums beat all around her, during a shamanic ceremony one summer solstice, she felt her head beginning to spin. Strange voices echoed all around her and she heard the sound of, what seemed like at least, a thousand horses. With that the floor opened up and she spiralled down a tunnel and found herself deep within the earth, in a cave. Here she saw a roaring fire and faces of the ancestors who had been waiting for her. As they held out their hands towards her she felt the most ecstatic rush flow up through her body and she began to shake internally. Her kundalini was awakening and she could feel each chakra energy point in her body pop. She then became aware that she was still dancing in ceremony to the beat of the drums, but feeling oh so alive and elated! Everything from sound, vision and feeling had a new clarity. Flavia had experienced dancing with the Divine through drum-induced euphoric trance dance.

The Shaman utilizes trance states through mental training and shamanic journeying. The more you practise, the deeper the trance becomes. During trance states the journey will feel similar to a daydream or a fantasy and you will start to question whether it is real or just your imagination. As you train yourself to go deeper and deeper you will find that these trance states feel as though they are taking place in your physical reality. The reason why a lot of people don't discover these stages of awareness is because the Middle World holds people in another form of trance, called illusion. This is cleverly designed to keep you in a deep trance of the undead. Neither alive or dead, asleep or awake, a journey through a thousand lifetimes of outer imaginary landscapes keeps you far beyond the Shaman's flight and within the limitations of the physical body.

The ancient mystics knew that ecstatic states of trance involve an experience of mystic self-transcendence; a Sufi dancer whirling into trance, the sacred marriage of call and response between African drummers and dancers, the raising of power of the Shaman's ability to bring forth and manifest the different forms of spirits and deities. The Hopi dresses as Kachinas and calls upon the spirits of all living things, including the ancestors who have died and become part of nature. By impersonating a Kachina the participant connects to the supernatural and embodies trance through dancing.

These soul flights, in whatever form they may take, are part of the trance state of learning to trust what is seen in the visions the Shamans receive.

Trance can be of varying degrees and duration depending on what tool is used to facilitate the journey. To become a Shaman one needs to experience union of both this reality and non-reality simultaneously. By entering into states of trance this can be obtained. The mastery of trance is to be able to walk the fine line grounded, centred and protected, but being able to read the messages, decipher the visions and embody all that is seen, felt and experienced in the soul flight.

If you wish to experience first-hand for yourself states of trance, ensure you have good people around you who have had first-hand experience of trance states. Make sure they know how to handle potential white-outs and retrieving the soul of a person who could disappear into the void, thus allowing another soul to take their body. This may sound scary, but for a fully experienced Shaman this comes with the territory. When you first experiment with trance you may find that you feel dizzy, your heart will beat faster, it may feel as though you are in a vortex or you may feel as though you are falling.

This is all part of going from a light trance, which is the beta state, into the alpha state of medium trance, to the deeper trance states of theta and delta. People who go into these trance states will feel as if their eyes are wide open, although to the onlooker they are shut. You may feel as if you are moving your head from side to side, but again to the onlooker you won't be. This is called being entranced with Spirit. Here you make your connection to spirit and take your soul flight, leaving your body behind to journey on a voyage of discovery to the lands of otherworldly realms in order to bring back information, wisdom and healing for yourself and others.

## 31

# Transmigration

It is a shamanic belief that when a person passes over their soul leaves the body and enters into another form, so that as souls we are continually reborn from life to life. Newborn babies are recognised as the souls of the ancestors. Tribes, such as those in Western Amazonia, avoid eating certain animals, including deer, because they believe ancestral souls have entered those animals' bodies.

Shamans also see and use transmigration as the transference of energies from one to another, of those who are living. A master will often hand down their knowledge, share their wisdom and make a gift of a treasured and sacred tool of theirs to a student or prodigy.

When Barbara was 12 years old the then Highland Seer, Swein Macdonald, took her under his wing up in the hills and woods of Inverness, Scotland. He taught and initiated her in the ways of nature, the Old Ways, the ancient art of divination, and guided her through ritual and ceremony. Nearing his death, many years later, Swein handed to her his trusty staff and seer stone, symbolising the gifts he had shared with and passed to her, as well as his title. Upon his passing Barbara took herself out on the land. As she stood with her back to a megalith and mourned for her old teacher she felt an incredible surge of spiritual energy jump into her crown chakra, at the top of her head, and calibrate throughout her entire body. Swein has continued to be her guide from thereon.

# 32

# Tree Spirits

Ancient and old, the standing ones have been with us since our beginning. They hold and support birds, animals and insects. They are the gateway through which we can traverse to the Lower and Upper Worlds of the gods and ancestors. They embody and support the sacred, and play a big part in our lives whether we are consciously aware of it or not.

Many shamanic tools are partly made of wood. From the drum to the flute, from the staff to rattles, they bring their spirit medicine into life with a beat, a breath, earthing to vibration, which calls to and assists us in our journey to connect with the spirits of the other worlds.

Trees are the lungs of the planet, providing us with the air that we breathe. A tree will exhale all that it does not need, and we as humans inhale all that the tree has extradited. In return, we breathe out that which the tree needs in order to live. One cannot live, or exist naturally, without the other. As we drive through the countryside and speed along motorways the tree spirits call to us from the roadside. But sadly too many people are wrapped up in their own worlds to notice. How many joggers and cyclists focus on end results, rather than acknowledging the trees they pass, for assisting in the purity of the air that they breathe in?

Those who walk in parks and forests will be more aware of the spirits of the trees. For it is near impossible not to feel their mighty presence. Do you feel excitement as the first buds of spring appear, and watch carefully as nature blossoms and grows to fullness and vitality into summer? How do you feel as autumn leaves become awash with splendid colour and fall to the ground? Do you feel the magic of stripped trees that stand naked and stark against the backdrop of the winter skyline? Trees show us how to walk with the natural world, to connect with the ebb and flow, to be part of the growth and to surrender to retreat. Do you have a favourite tree? Do the tree spirits call to you when you are out in nature? Sense when it is time to plant your seeds in order to blossom and grow. The next time you are out in nature allow yourself to be guided by the tree spirits. As you walk along, ask them for guidance. Perhaps you need healing or support, spells or psychic protection. Within every tree spirit resides the medicine to help you through life's journey.

Once a tree spirit has called to you, you will feel compelled to go and sit under it. Before doing so ensure that you ask permission to enter the tree's sacred space, and that of its residents. It's important to bring an offering for the tree spirits, as you would do when connecting with any spirit of nature, such as seeds or nuts. This ensures that the cycle of life is continuous.

Sit with your back leaning against the tree's trunk. Breathe with the tree, become as one with its spirit. You might feel yourself falling backwards into the tree, just allow this natural process to happen and become the tree. Feel its roots going deep into the earth, connecting you to the Lower World. This is the place to ground your energies, to root you. Then make your way back up to the trunk and feel how solid your connection to the Middle World is. This is where you centre yourself. Continue way up into the branches, reaching up into the Upper World. This is your place of protection. Feel your arms reaching up into the skies, connecting to the spirits that reside there. Become the tree as you connect with the Upper, Middle and Lower Worlds simultaneously. Then take your hands over your heart and feel the tree spirit energy flowing through you.

When you are finished, give thanks by leaving your offerings around the tree. Take a mental picture of your tree and breathe in the essence of the tree spirit. Make a note in your journal of all that you felt and experienced. To be one with the tree spirits is to awaken the spirit within you.

Currently we have more than 400 billion trees on our planet, all breathing for us. That is 60 trees per person! There are more than 23,000 different types of trees in the world, each embracing their individual medicine. Below is a short list of trees that have called to us, and the meanings of the medicine they hold. As custodians of the Earth we have a responsibility to the tree spirits. And, in turn, each one is waiting for us to discover and tap in to all that they have to offer. Let us no longer ignore our tree brothers and sisters, and instead learn to connect and work together with them to bring about balance and harmony from their meaning and message:

**Alder:** Gives you the power and desire to make your own way in the world. Time to fight your own battles; nobody will stand in your way. This is the tree of journeying, self-confidence, bravery, supervisory skills, and spiritual growth. Wear an amulet of alder for psychic protection. Your strength and passion will endure through all the hard times you will face.

**Apple:** Ensures love will surround you, see the beauty that lives within you. Be generous with your gifts. The apple is symbolic of fertility, peace, plenty, and joy. Apple aids in the propagation of skills and is often used in love or fertility ceremonies. It promotes peace, harmony and visions. Your truth will set you free to live in beauty and honesty.

**Ash:** Signifies great wisdom calls to you to surrender and connect to the ancient way. Time to awaken great strength and might, to assist you in your work. Ash is excellent for increasing mental focus and balance, communication, intelligence, wisdom, and curiosity. Use ash to remove mental blockages and aid in understanding. Time for your soul growth, expansion and self-renewal.

**Beech:** Denotes that your patience and tolerance with others is an example of true spirit. You have let go of fixed ideas and have learnt from the past. Now is a time for you to enjoy pure pleasure and desire in all you wish. Magic and divination surround you. Take time out to read, study and understand the wheel of the year.

**Birch:** Indicates new beginnings and renewal of youthful joy to awake you. Time to go on a journey where no-one has gone before. Time to take root in new souls and new lands. It's time to shine your light so others may follow your example. Light the fire in your heart and allow your spark of passion to drive you forwards to your end goals.

**Cedar:** Calls to you to rise like the phoenix from the Underworld, renewed and cleansed. Build yourself strong foundations that will last a lifetime. Clear away all negativity from your home, your work and yourself. It is time to create your sacred space with ceremonies of protection. Deep healing will ensue.

**Cherry Blossom:** Means good fortune calls to you from the mists of time. It is time to ground your energy and become centred as you face any obstacles. Your intuitive insights will help you focus on your visions and dreams. Rebirth of the old you, new beginnings abound.

**Elder:** Suggests personal evolution is assured through your continuation to transition fears and doubts into positive energies. By banishing those who no longer serve your highest purpose, you change your energy. Awakening healing abilities within allows you to change the cycles, thus promoting good health and fortitude.

**Elm:** Encourages inner strength so you rise with the sap of life. Feel it flowing in your blood, renewing and invigorating your very being. Your endurance will carry you forward soon to a new path. It is time to plant seeds and cultivate your garden. Allow your spiritual fertility to spread through the written word.

**Hawthorn:** Brings focus on inner relationships. Others will try to contradict and stop what you are doing. Stand strong and face the consequences of others' actions towards you. Increase your self-confidence by removing all negative thoughts that have come from other people. Take the time to nurture patience, for this will assist you in the work to come.

**Hazel:** Shows how your creativity of words speaks a story of purity and honesty in all you do. Your artistic abilities call to you to paint a picture through song, chant, dance movement and laughter. Your magical knowledge of life calls to you from who you have been, and to open up to wisdom, creativity, intelligence, and divination.

**Holly:** Demonstrates always to follow right actions and right deeds. It is time to purify yourself of anger through a sacred ceremony of fire. Remove your barriers that have been put in place, by yourself, to protect you from others. Time to transfer and reclaim your personal power that others have taken from you, until now!

**Horse Chestnut:** Asks you to seize the moment. All your harvesting of ideas has come to fruition. Gather all the supplies you will need, for you are about to embark upon a great journey. Provision has been made for you to survive and grow through life's spiritual journey. Prepare, gather and then rejoice in the bountiful opportunities that bloom.

**Oak:** Reminds you that your nobility and birthright gives you stability and strength to rise above all indiscretions. Seek the truth and stand strong through all things. Oak represents truth, steadfast knowledge and protection. Centre your mind and still the monkey chatter, allowing you to focus on the task at hand, while ignoring distractions. Observe and watch!

**Poplar:** Indicates victory is at hand; time to shape-shift your visions into reality. Have hope for what is about to come and carry this with you always. Journey into the dreamtime, paying attention to what you see there. Lost and forgotten memories will return. Though life is hard at times you can endure this by keeping your roots strong.

**Rowan:** Suggests it's time to express yourself and connect with nature. Rowan asks that you protect yourself at all times. Bring balance into your life between the worlds. Seek out new teachings and ways of connecting to Spirit. Climb high; ask questions until you get the correct answers. Don't settle for anything less.

**Scots Fir:** Encourages you to harness your energy, you will achieve clarity and focus for what you need to do. Ancient wisdom calls to you from the Summerlands, as the ancestors await your remembrance. It is time to go on your vision quest. Sit in nature and reach for the stars. The tree spirits whisper to you great teachings and wisdom.

**Sycamore:** Indicates the universe wishes to gift you with intuitive and spiritual gifts of abundance. Enjoy the nourishment and beauty that surrounds you. It is important not to forget or put aside those talents and abilities you have already. It is time to walk the sacred wheel of the year and draw on nature to teach and support you.

**Willow:** Asks you to trust your imagination, intuition, and inner visions as they guide you forward. Your strong will enables you to focus on the matter at heart. You have learnt from the past and now journey on your soul-flight towards change. Your wishes will come true, fulfilling your destiny. Never give up no matter what!

**Yew:** Tells you to step out of the illusion that has been created by society and those around you. Rites of passage call to you to reclaim the fragments of your soul, lost and taken away from you by others. Transference is at hand. Stand your ground. Seek solitude within the Great Mystery. It is time for introspection and silence.

# About the Authors

Barbara Meiklejohn-Free is the UK's best loved and hardest working 'Wisdom Keeper' – teacher, advocate and protector of the great Earth-centred traditions. She offers mediumship, shamanic healing, rebirthing, soul retrieval, past life regression and rites of passage, combining them all together in her readings and raising them to new levels of awareness in order to help people become aware of who they are and why they are here. Best-selling author Barbara also leads people on guided site visits across the globe to meet the native people, to gain an understanding first-hand of the way they live according to the teachings of Mother Earth. She worked at the Arthur Findlay College and teaches at the College of Psychic Studies in London. **www.spiritvisions.co.uk**

Flavia Kate Peters is an author, speaker, therapist, and a natural mystic. Known as 'The Faery Shaman', Flavia Kate works closely with the nature spirits and faeries. She offers readings and guidance as well as giving talks and workshops at events and shows throughout the year. She is a Reiki and Crystal Master, Angel Therapist® and a spiritual counsellor. Flavia Kate is a regular columnist for FAE Magazine and teaches her popular Angel Energy Practitioner® certification programme worldwide. **www.flaviakatepeters.com**

MOON

BOOKS

Moon Books invites you to begin or deepen your encounter with Paganism, in all its rich, creative, flourishing forms.